THE
KINGDOM PARABLES

DISPENSATIONALLY

AND

PRACTICALLY CONSIDERED

David Boyd Long

JOHN RITCHIE LTD
CHRISTIAN PUBLICATIONS

40 Beansburn, Kilmarnock, Scotland

ISBN 0-946351-69-4

Copyright © 1997 by John Ritchie Ltd.
40 Beansburn, Kilmarnock, Scotland

Typeset by John Ritchie Ltd., Kilmarnock
Printed by Bell & Bain Ltd., Glasgow

Foreword

All too easily we accept the trite sayings so many quote unthinkingly, "Parables are earthly stories with a heavenly meaning". And perhaps for that reason we relegate parables to the curriculum of Sunday School and fail to recognise why our Lord used parables and therefore, if for no other reason, no one should underestimate the importance of the parables He told.

Contrary to popular opinion it may be, but we should acknowledge that the Lord told parables not to illustrate heavenly truths by earthly stories. According to Matt 13:11-15 the use of parables was in line with God's governmental dealings with Israel, that to him that hath might be given and from him that hath not might be taken away even that which he had. Thus there were those to whom it was given to know the mysteries of the kingdom of heaven and others who seeing saw not and hearing heard not neither did they understand just as Isa 6:9-10 had foretold.

There were occasions when our Lord's opponents might perceive that He spake a parable against them (Matt 21:45; Mark 12:12; Luke 20:19) but they did not have the key to unlock His teaching. The parable of the sower or the parable of the good Samaritan was not more accessible to them than the others He told. But each should be accessible to every saint of God for each has the enlightening of the Spirit.

To us then it is given to understand parables. And with the enlightenment of the Spirit we are equipped to absorb their teaching that we might be intelligent Christians. The neglected teaching of the parables would preserve from many of the pitfalls around us today. The parable of the mustard seed, for example, would preserve from the promoting of the big and impressive that offers much to the very birds of the air.

David Long's rich experience of christian life and service equips him well to set out the teaching of the parables and their application to his readers. Few would mistake the shepherd heart that longs that young and old would mine the rich seam represented in the kingdom and other parables. All will find his analysis of the parables careful and perceptive; all will find his analysis of Christendom equally considered and perceptive; all with any measure of humility will find his applications pertinent.

I am pleased to commend this book to a wide readership. It makes no pretence to weigh the many arguments of the past or to expound every facet of the Lord's many parables. But as only a spiritual brother can, prayerfully and earnestly David Long has committed to permanent form helpful outlines of precious truths from which all can profit.

Tom Wilson

Contents

Preface

Over sixty years ago two little books came into my life. They were second-hand, but as a young believer they opened up a whole new understanding of the Gospels, especially in relation to the different ways or dispensations in which God has dealt with and tested man. They became cherished and life-long friends, accompanying me to Africa and around the world, and although a little worse for wear they are still with me and often consulted or re-read.

One of these little volumes of only 160 pages bears the title *On the Sermon on the Mount* by C.F. Hogg and J.B. Watson, Pickering and Inglis, 1933. The other, even smaller and only one quarter of an inch thick, *The Parables of our Lord and What They Teach*, published by G. Morrish of London, has no author's name but the style marks it as the work of the saintly J.G. Bellett, and though it has no date it would have been published between 1860 and 1865. Both these books are long out of print, hard to find second-hand, and when some publishers were approached about reprinting the older book they were too busy with modern eye catchers. Two other books, one *Matthew's Gospel* by E.W. Rodgers and the other *Dispensationalism To-day* by C.C. Ryrie, Moody Press, Chicago have also been a great help to the present writer who gladly acknowledges his debt to all four, and no doubt some echoes from them will come through in the present studies.

Through the years there have been quite a few books written on the subject of the parables of our Lord by authors of repute like Trench, Habershon, Taylor and others, but most of these are also out of print, and some might prove heavy reading because of poor organization of the material. One has a wealth of excellent material which is treated in such a way that the reader has to turn to a very detailed index which will send him to five or six different parts of the large volume to find all the teaching on that subject in one parable, a process which few would have the patience to do. Others seem to treat the parables as devotional sermonettes on moral teaching without much helpful overall view or meaningful context.

The parables have also suffered a lot from being used as texts for gospel messages with little regard for the reason for the giving of the parables in the first place, or its contextual significance. Examples of this latter would be "The ten virgins", "The good Samaritan", or "The sheep and the goats", where many seem to see little beyond a gospel text.

The subject of the "Mysteries of the Kingdom of Heaven" is to-day largely neglected, misunderstood, or misapplied and, as a result, quite a few simply ignore it as being either too complex or not very important. We believe that, if properly understood, they are not only free of complexity, but also throw light on much of the rest of the NT. This teaching, particularly as connected with the Kingdom Parables, can never be properly grasped except in the context of what leads up to them.

The present unpretentious little volume is an attempt at making these matters simple for younger or newer believers.

David B. Long
Ballygowan, N. Ireland
July 1997

CHAPTER 1

Introduction to the Subject

The writer of Matthew's Gospel was obviously a Jew, as seen in his many OT references and quotations, his constant allusions to Jewish history, customs, and ceremonies, and his references to and quotations from OT prophetic writings. As one of the Lord's intimate companions, he was well aware that his fellow-countrymen and their leaders had emphatically rejected Jesus as Messiah and King, indeed had brutally crucified Him with every mark of hatred and contempt. His followers were persecuted cruelly, even to the death, yet Matthew, in an attempt at putting the record straight, boldly opens his treatise with the words "The genealogy of Jesus the Messiah", "Christ" being simply the Greek translation of the Hebrew word "Messiah".

This genealogy shows Jesus to be the direct descendent of Abraham, thus having legal claim to the land of Israel. It also shows that He was the lineal descendant of David, the first king of Israel actually chosen by God, thus making Him rightful heir to the throne of Israel.

Matthew also shows that not only His genealogy was right, but also His place of birth, the slaughter by Herod of the children, the flight to Egypt, the dwelling in Nazareth, etc. All these events fulfilled the OT prophecies given as the signs by which Messiah could be recognised when He came. They can all be found with an ordinary reference Bible. The ministry of John Baptist is cited by Matthew as the fulfilment of the clear and specific prophecy of Isaiah 40:3. In the first three chapters of this Gospel there are seven prophetic passages cited or referred to which the writer shows were fulfilled by the Lord.

Matthew proceeds to show that this Jesus the Messiah proved Himself invulnerable to any Satanic attack or temptation; that He performed all the validating miracles prophetically promised for this glorious coming one. Then in chs. 5-7 we have the Lord Himself in the Sermon on the Mount giving an outline of the characteristics of His kingdom and the spirit of those under His rule.

Some would have us see this kingdom of heaven as something for Israel, and pertaining to the future millennial kingdom. A moment's thought will surely answer such an argument. How can the background conditions of the Sermon on the mount ever exist in that perfect kingdom of the future? Here the king is absent and his servants "persecuted and reviled for righteousness sake", a situation inconceivable when Christ rules on the throne of His father David and righteousness will prevail. Here an unjust judge refuses to hear the plea of a widow with an enemy who has wronged her, while Christ's future reign will be one of equity and no unjust judge will be in a place of power, neither will there be a persecuting enemy to maltreat the believer. Here there is a danger of the salt losing its savour; surely impossible then. Here they are warned against adultery, cursing a brother, putting away a wife, in danger of being slapped on the cheek, of being sued at law and their very clothing seized; they may fast, lose riches laid up on earth, they are urged to enter by the straight gate, are warned against false teachers and false profession. Any such conditions which would be unthinkable in the millennial kingdom.

The argument is also brought forward that to-day we are in the church and not the kingdom, but perhaps we need to remind ourselves that in Col 1:13 our salvation is equated with being liberated from the power (authority or kingdom) of darkness and "translated into the kingdom of His dear son". Rom 14:7 says, "The kingdom of God is not meat and drink; but righteousness, and peace, and joy in the Holy Spirit." In Rev 1:9 John identifies himself as "your brother and companion in tribulation and in the kingdom and patience of Jesus Christ". Then significantly we are told in Acts 1:3 that between the resurrection and ascension of our Lord the theme of His instructions to the disciples was "the things pertaining to the kingdom of God". In the same book of Acts 14:22, 19:8, 28:23,31 Paul's preaching is on the same theme both to Gentiles and Jews even after he warned the latter that he was turning from them to the Gentiles. These and quite a few other NT Scriptures speak clearly about the believer of the present age being in the kingdom, albeit a kingdom in mystery, of which we shall say more later. Indeed every epistle in the NT refers to believers as in this kingdom with the exception of Philippians, Titus, and those of John. E.W. Rodgers puts it neatly when he says that "Believers in the present era are seen in the Body as to privilege, as children of God as to relationship, and in the kingdom as to responsibility".

Though related, this kingdom and the church are quite distinct, the former embracing the larger area of profession, while the latter is the true body of Christ as seen by God. The latter is within the former yet seen as something very special. Perhaps a little illustration from the OT might help toward an understanding of this.

In 1 Samuel, King Saul was on the throne although doomed to destruction by God, and another king had been secretly anointed, "a man after God's own heart". This was David, the God-anointed king, but he was rejected and persecuted by Saul and all his followers, indeed David was hidden at the cave Adullam and elsewhere in obscurity while the masses followed the doomed king Saul. A large group of men, said to be in debt and discontented, came to David saying, "Thine are we, David, son of Jesse" and they later grew to a great company over which David became "captain" or commander-in-chief.

They were, in effect, a little kingdom within a kingdom, though their lord, while anointed, was not yet crowned. By faith they looked forward to that "crowning day" which was still in the future. So to-day God has a kingdom made up of those who have "confessed Jesus Christ as Lord" while "the prince of this world" and his followers ride high, rejecting God's king and those who acknowledge Him. The rejectors of Christ rule the world, while those who wait in faith for the return and crowning of the true king are ignored or in some places persecuted. We are indeed in a kingdom, though it is in "mystery" form, and the king is absent.

So in Matthew's Gospel, Jesus the Christ is presented as fulfilling all the prophecies, showing all the promised characteristics, demonstrating His unique power over all the tactics of Satan, over sicknesses, evil spirits, winds and waves, and even death itself as in the case of the son of the widow of Nain, and Lazarus.

In chs. 5-7 the Lord outlines what E.W. Rodgers calls the platform on which He proposes to establish His kingdom and the character of those who make it up. This would be "not in word (that is not in mere talk or profession), but in power"; "not meat and drink (regulations and ceremonies) but in righteousness, and peace, and joy in the Holy Spirit". Then He is shown as preaching or announcing the kingdom of which He is the Messiah or anointed king, later sending His disciples to do the same thing. Up to this point the offer of the kingdom is to "the lost sheep of the house of Israel", indeed the messengers were ordered not to go into "the way of the Gentiles".

The offer was rejected, John saying that "He came unto His own and His own received him not", while in Luke He is hurried out of the synagogue in an attempt to throw Him off the cliff, and in Matthew He upraids Chorazin,

Bethsaida, and Capernaum for refusing His message reinforced by miracles which, had they been done in Sodom, would have led to its salvation. Matthew follows this growing rejection in more detail, since he in a special way presents Christ as king. From ch.10 of his Gospel onwards the attitude of the nation's leaders toward their Messiah becomes more and more antagonistic and aggressive as they dog Christ's footsteps, criticise His actions, contradict His teachings, and then go about seeking ways to destroy Him.

Being thus rejected by "His own" a great change becomes clearly noticeable in His message and ministry for here we are watching the coming foreshadowing of a new dispensation, and this word calls for some remarks.

What is a dispensation?

This word frightens some who think of it as a profound theological term for scholars only. Others reject or even denounce it because it clashes with some of their firmly-held ideas. These sometimes use the argument that because the word *dispensation* is not in the Bible it is either untrue or unimportant. This is, of course, a mistake for the word occurs at least five times in the NT though not always translated as "dispensation". The Greek scholars tell us that the original word *oikonomia* is a compound of "house" *(oikos)* and "law or rule" *(nomos)*. This is the origin of our word "economy" in the sense of a period of government under some specific principle or philosophy. W.E. Vine says that it is used for the administration of a property or house, usually by a steward. *The Dictionary of Religious Terms* says, among other things, that it is "a term for a period of history during which God deals in a specific way with men".

The Dispensation of Innocence

We see without difficulty the great change which took

place in God's dealings with man between Genesis 2 and what immediately follows. In the beginning God rejoiced in His creation, calling it "very good". There is communion and free communication between God and man, the former seeing man's need of a companion, making for him a helper suitable (meet), since in the animal creation no such companion existed. There is no barrier between man and God and no need for sacrifice. It is the age or dispensation of innocence for there is no sin, no barrier, no distance, and God walks with man in the garden in complete harmony.

The Dispensation of Conscience

With the entrance of sin there is an abrupt change. Man is found skulking among the trees, conscious of his violation of the Creator's administrative rule and law. He is driven out of the garden of Eden, the way back barred by a flaming sword, and all his children are born in that outside place. If man now wishes to approach God he must do so on the ground of a blood sacrifice. This indicates a clear-cut change of administration. Man became conscious of his sin and clearly indicated this by trying to cover his shame with an apron of leaves. Abel "by faith" brings an approach offering and is accepted. We emphasise the words "by faith" as in Heb 11:4 because "faith cometh by hearing, and hearing by the word of God" (Rom 10:17), showing us that Abel did not reason this out and invent the way back himself. He had instruction from God as to the new rule or dispensation of God, and accepted it. This is the beginning of the dispensation of conscience. Adam and Eve had a conscience of sin when they tried to hide and invent a covering for their need. Abel must have had a consciousness of sin to bring a sacrifice to cover his sin and make approach to God possible.

By Genesis 6, approximately 1500 years later, man's

conscience had become so seared and callused that he had lost all fear of God or sense of his own wickedness, and therefore of the need for approach to God through sacrifice: "Every imagination of the thoughts of his heart was only evil continually" (Gen 6:5). Since conscience had failed as a bridle on man, God was now driven to the drastic measure of destroying all with the Flood, preserving only Noah and his wife with their three sons and their wives. The dispensation of conscience had ended in failure and judgement.

The Dispensation of Human Government

After the flood God dealt with man under a new administration or dispensation; that of human government. Noah and his successors are given complete sovereignty over the animal creation and they are now, apparently for the first time, permitted to eat animal flesh, though not blood. Then in Gen 9:6 the Lord adds: "Whoso sheddeth man's blood, by man shall his blood be shed". Man's life is sacred since he is said to be created in the image of God, therefore under human government the murderer is to be put to death. A covenant is then established between God and man in these terms, and the rainbow, a visible reminder to man of this covenant, is given in the very heavens. This is a new departure and a new framework, for before the flood Noah could "preach righteousness" (2 Pet 2:5), but he did not bear the sword and had no authority to enforce righteousness or even law and order.

This dispensation of human government ended in failure, indeed it was doomed to failure since in a short time from its initiation Noah himself failed in drunkenness and shame, and one of his own sons is put under a curse. All this only about 700 years after the flood, and at the end of it we find in Gen 11:4 those under human government gathering with a plan all of their own. They would make brick in place of stone and slime instead of mortar, which was not a promising start from any viewpoint, but then there never was rock of any kind in that area. They would then build themselves a city and a tower which would reach to heaven, thus bonding themselves together in a confederation which could not be broken or its constituent parts scattered and weakened. It was to be a sort of United Nations or European Union of that day, and its name was to be Babel which would later turn into Babylon. God came down and blew on their whole arrogant scheme, confounding their language, and instead of binding themselves together against whatever plans God may have had, they were scattered in every direction. Thus ended the dispensation of human government.

The Dispensation of Israel as the chosen race

This brings us to an entirely new thing in God's ways of dealing with man. In Romans 1, we read that because of their incorrigible idolatry and moral depravity God "gave (the nations) up...gave them up...gave them over". With this treble affirmation of doom we read that it affected them in body, soul, and spirit. Read carefully that they "dishonoured their bodies" (v.24), perverted "their affections" in sodomy (v.26), were given over to a "reprobate mind" (v.28).

At this point God introduces a totally new thing in His ways of dealing with man, when in Genesis 12 He selects and calls out a man named Abram from the very area of the tower of Babel and moves him away over to a land which He promises to give to him and to his descendants. This man will become the father of a completely new nation, and from that nation one would be born in whom all the families of earth would be blessed. So now one man, and one nation springing from him, will be God's special channel, and His instrument for the bringing of

His plans to fruition. This is an entirely new departure and surely the beginning of a new dispensation. Because of God's dealings with Abram's grandson Jacob (who got a new name – Israel) this whole nation came to be called Israel. To this nation in due time God sent the Messiah, the promised one, the King, the Saviour – His own eternally co-equal Son. Much, however, was to happen before that.

In Exodus 12 the nation which sprang from Abraham was liberated, redeemed, and set on their way toward the land promised to their forefather, "the friend of God". When they reached Mount Sinai, God entered into a solemn covenant with them, to the conditions of which they all too readily consented with the words, "All that the Lord hath said we will do". Some see this as the beginning of a new dispensation of law and there is room for difference of opinion here. Since, however, even at Sinai God is still working within the framework of the Abrahamic covenant and his descendants as promised in that covenant the present writer finds it difficult to split it into two eras or dispensations, seeing it rather as one, the dispensation of Israel as the chosen race. The nations, or Gentiles, had long ago been given up, though even in this God would in grace make provision for them.

God's plan looks forward to ultimate blessing on offer to the whole world: "In thee shall all the families of the earth be blessed" (Acts 3:25 with Gen 12:3). This promised seed did come, as we have mentioned above, but the nation rejected Him and the kingdom which He had offered them.

CHAPTER 2

The Great Crisis

We have noted that, being rejected by "His own" (John 1:11), our Lord's messages take on a totally different tone; He turns as the passage in John shows, "to as many as [would receive] Him". The tension has been building, but from here on, the breaking point is quickly reached.

In Matt 11:1-15 in fulfilment of prophecies by both Isaiah and Malachi the Lord authenticates as His forerunner John Baptist, at this time in prison and shortly to be beheaded. He then goes on to liken the behaviour of His own nation to that of petulant and perverse children who refuse to be satisfied, no matter how many different approaches may be taken to win them. He supposes a suggested game of weddings at which the offer to play the pipes if the others will dance is met with refusal. Another proposal is offered: "Well, let's play funerals in which we'll be the mourners and you can do the lamenting", but this too is rejected. The Lord is saying that John was a man of the desert with a message of doom, yet they would not give ear, while He, the Lord Jesus, mingled with them, helped them, and preached grace and love. They would listen to neither the one nor the other.

The Lord then becomes more severe in His condemnation of the villages around His actual home town where He had been openly rejected – Chorazin, Bethsaida, and Capernaum. He reminds them that if Tyre, Sidon, or even Sodom had seen the miracles which they had seen they would have repented long ago and, He added, in the day of judgment it would be much easier for these corrupt and idolatrous cities than for these which He Himself had visited in grace. This is the first reference to a judgment day for Israel for spurning their rightful king *Emmanuel* (God with us). At the same time He gives more than a hint of turning to those who would hear Him saying, "Come unto me all ye that labour and are heavy laden and I will give you rest." In the words of John, if "His own received Him not" He would turn to "as many" as would.

In Matt 12:14 the leaders of the nation "held council against Him how they might destroy Him". Note that killing Him would not be enough. They wanted to kill Him by crucifixion so that He would never be honoured or respected by anyone. How very wrong they were! The word "destroy" here is the same word as used in 2:13 of what Herod wanted to do to Him as an infant. Later in the same chapter they accuse Him of doing miracles by Satanic power, and after that when they goaded Him with a request for a sign (miracle) He bluntly informs them that there would be no more sign miracles except "the sign of the prophet Jonah", that is the sign of His resurrection. Jonah had been three days and three nights in the bowels of the great fish, so He would be the same time in the grave. The door is closed in their faces.

A short time after this in vv.46-50 of the same chapter, Matthew gives us a clear hint of the dispensational break. While our Lord yet talked to His followers in the house, His mother and brothers are announced as "standing outside" wishing to speak with Him. We do not know what prompted this sudden intrusion. Perhaps they wished to warn Him of the dangers surrounding Him, or of the Sanhedrin's decision to have Him destroyed, or even to have Him get away from such a danger zone, and of course we do not need to know. Instead of going to them He gestures to His disciples and says, "Behold my mother and my brethren"; they were His brethren along with all those who will "do the will of [His] father." If one asks what the will of the Father is, the answer is not far to seek, for Christ has already told us that it is "that all men should honour the Son even as they honour the Father" who said, "In [Him] I have found all my delight."

Of one thing we may be sure. In the light of Christ's care for Mary in the last moments of His agony on the cross, His response to her was neither intentionally harsh or rude. It was rather a symbolic way of warning those around Him that a new order was about to be established based on spiritual rather than human relationships. He had even warned the disciples a short time before that those accepting their message would find that "a man's enemies would be those of his own household". God had indeed other plans. The story of the keepers of the master's vineyard shows how that enmity would develop: because of their rebellion and murder of the owner's son everything would be taken from them and given to others while they would be "miserably destroyed".

The word "parable" is not found in Matthew's Gospel up to this point, and it seems clear that these parables are based squarely on Israel's rejection of her anointed king. That rejection was not only emphatic, but violent and murderous. It was also not a movement initiated by a rabble of louts and troublemakers. As we have already seen the plot to destroy Jesus was taken by the Sanhedrin which was made up of the leaders – the high-priestly family, scribes (teachers), Pharisees, and Saducees. The Lord Himself emphasised this in the story of husbandmen of the vineyard when they said, "We will not have this man to rule over us." It was fulfilled when the Jerusalem crowd chanted in the presence of the Roman oppressor, "Crucify Him; we have no king but Caesar", and again, "His blood be on us and on our children." The last words of ch. 12 and those which open ch. 13 are very significant. (There is of course no chapter division in the original text.)

In the former, as we have noticed, He indicated that a whole new structure of relationships was being unveiled based not on human and family ties but on individual commitment to Himself and His gospel. He had already warned them that such commitment could even divide between father and son, mother and daughter, and that a man's enemies might well become those of his own household (Matt 10:34-39).

Then ch.13 opens with the significant words, "*The same day* went Jesus out of the house and *sat by the seaside* and great multitudes were gathered together unto him, so that he *went into a ship* and sat; and the whole multitude sat on the shore. And He spoke many things unto them in parables."

To the careful reader of Holy Scripture (and we should all be such) the steps are clearly emphasised and intended to impress. He "leaves the house" – Israel is consistently called "the house of Israel" as well as "my house", "this house" etc. in both Old and New Testaments. In Ezekiel 9,10 we have a vivid description of God's withdrawal of Himself and His glory from "the house", meaning in the first place the temple but including the whole nation. Later our Lord was to say "Your house is left unto you desolate (deserted)" (Matt 13:38; Luke 13:35). So here the act is symbolic; He leaves the house; goes to the seaside, often a picture of the restless Gentile nations, and even pushes out "into the waters" from which position He addresses the people in parables.

CHAPTER 3

The Significance
of Parabolic Teaching

This appears to have been our Lord's first use of parables in this way. Matthew does not even refer to or use the word "parable" until ch. 13 and even the other two synoptic Gospels show the same pattern. All attemped "harmonisations" of the Gospels agree at least on one thing, i.e. that Matthew 13 slots into Mark 4 and Luke 8. In Mark there is only one mention of a parable before this which is in 3:23 and is not related to the kingdom but is simply, "How can Satan cast out Satan?" In Luke the same pattern is seen. Before ch. 8 the writer refers only twice to "a parable" and again it is to a completely different type of subject. In 5:36 it is "no man putteth a piece of a new garment on an old"; in 6:39 it is "Can the blind lead the blind? Shall they not both fall into the ditch?" This seems to make it clear that prior to this period which is given in detail in Matthew 13 parabolic teaching does not appear to have been used by our Lord. It was a new departure.

This is further emphasised when the startled disciples asked, "Why speakest thou unto them in parables?" Most of us have heard it said that a parable is "an earthly story with a heavenly meaning" and this may well be so. It has also been said that the Lord used them to help His hearers by simplifying His teaching by little stories in everyday terms, but this is simply not so. His answer must have startled them even more, and may do the same to those holding the common view of the subject. His reply was,

"Because it is given unto *you* to understand the mysteries of the Kingdom of Heaven, but to *them* (the rejectors) it is not given...and in them is fulfilled the prophecy of Esaias which saith, By hearing ye shall hear and not (in no wise) understand" (vv.11-17).

So the master has made it clear that the parabolic method was *not* to simplify so that the multitudes could understand, but rather to show that since they had rejected Him and His word He had no further message or teaching for them but that of judgment and doom. This runs parallel to His reply at the same time when they asked Him for another sign. His reply was, "There shall no sign be given [them] but the sign of the prophet Jonah", which assertion we have already explained. On the other hand He will patiently explain the mysteries of the new kingdom to His disciples (v.18); its character, its methods, the behaviour of its subjects in the absence of the king but in the light of His return, and the rewards for faithful service at the time of that return. Perhaps it should also be pointed out that the word "mystery" as used in the NT does not mean something simply mystical, enigmatic, or difficult. It is from a Greek word *musterion* which we are told means "something formerly hidden and secret but now revealed", especially to the initiated.

So, to summarise this subject we might say again that while the church and the kingdom are to be distinguished they are not to be seen as unrelated. The kingdom is seen as broader and embracing the whole sphere of profession in which wheat and tares continue to grow together "in the field" (which the Lord Himself identified as "the world") until the time when the master separates them and burns the tares. In the kingdom there are good fish and bad, wise virgins and foolish, and so on. In the kingdom there are also those who go on for a time and then are choked out by "the cares of this age" or those who spring up quickly but have no depth of root and so shortly they wither and die. In the church, which is His body and which is seen by God in its spiritual oneness past, present, and future, none of the above is true, though it may be seen in measure in the local church which has been committed to men.

If anyone should still insist "the kingdom" in this mystery sense does not refer to us or to the present age, then the question must be asked, "What kingdom is it and who is in it?" It is not Israel for that kingdom was destroyed in AD 70 and 130; the people scattered, set aside, blinded, a veil on their hearts; the branches of the olive tree cut off – not recognised by God, called by Him "Not my people".

Neither can it be the kingdom on earth in manifest and visible glory, for that takes place after the Rapture and the Tribulation when Christ takes the throne of His father David. In that kingdom there can be no Satanic influence for he will be shut up in the abyss for the whole period. Therefore there will be no snatching away of good seed, no sowing of tares, no persecution of the godly by the wicked, no unjust judges, all of which and more are experienced in the kingdom as seen in Matt 5-6-7 as well as in the kingdom parables. Neither can it be the "everlasting kingdom" of the eternal state where, unlike the kingdom outlined in the Sermon on the Mount and in the parables, there is no sin, no pain, no tears, no night, no failure in service and where, we are told in Rev 22:3, "the throne of God and of the Lamb are in it". Outside these we know of no other kingdom, so we ask again, "To what kingdom are the objectors referring in reference to these parables of the kingdom?"

CHAPTER 4

An Outline of the Five Groups of Kingdom Parables

To focus and simplify these parables, and to give some sort of orderly framework on which to work, we suggest dividing them into five groups. This writer finds it easier to grapple with a complex study if it can be organised into meaningful sections.

Group 1
Three parables dealing with the rejection of Israel.
1. Matt 21:28. The two sons. Failure in Obedience.
2. Matt 21:33. The vineyard, and its husbandmen. Failure in Fidelity.
3. Luke 13:6. The fruitless fig tree. Failure in Fruit-bearing.
Two others overlap somewhat with these but because of added features we leave them for a fuller treatment in Group 3. They are: The marriage of the king's son (Matt 22:2); The great supper (Luke 14:16).

Group 2
Eight parables dealing with God's ways in setting up the kingdom and Satan's ways of opposing.
1. Matt 13:3. The sower, and the seed.
2. Mark 4:26. Growth of the seed.
3. Matt 13:24. The wheat and the tares.
4. Matt 13:31; Mark 4:30; Luke 13:18. The mustard seed.
5. Matt 13:33; Luke 13:20. Three measures of meal.

6. Matt 13:44. The hidden treasure.
7. Matt 13:45. The goodly pearl.
8. Matt 13:47. The dragnet.

Group 3
Seven parables concerning God's ways of bringing men into the kingdom.
1. Luke 15:3. The lost sheep; Luke 15:8. The lost coin; Luke 15:22. The lost son.
2. Matt 22:2. The marriage supper of the king's son.
3. Luke 14:16. The great supper.
4. Luke 18:10. Two men before God.
5. Luke 7:41. The two debtors.
6. Matt 20:1. The labourers and their rewards.
7. Luke 18:1. The unjust judge.

Group 4
Seven parables concerning responsibilities of the subjects of the kingdom.
1. Luke 10:30. The compassionate Samaritan.
2. Luke 12:16. The wealthy planner.
3. Luke 16:1. The unjust steward.
4. Matt 18:23. The unmerciful servant.
5. Matt 25:14. The talents.
6. Luke 19:12. The pounds.
7. Luke 14:7. The guests at the feast.

Group 5
One parable giving a prophetic survey of the development of whole age.
Matt 25:1. The ten virgins.

CHAPTER 5

Group 1 Parables
The Rejection of Israel

Group 1 Parable 1:

The Two Sons   Matt 21:28-32

Context is extremely important in understanding any Scripture and none more so than in the parables of our Lord. Those connected with the setting aside of Israel were not the first parables recorded but they must be studied first if we are to understand the historical and moral setting of each.

Matthew 21 begins with Christ's final approach to His capital city of Jerusalem. He comes riding on a donkey in fulfilment of Zech 9:9, "Behold thy king cometh unto thee, meek and sitting upon an ass." He did not come as the Assyrians, Babylonians, Greeks, and Romans had come with massed armies to crush or subjugate. He came as their own king who had shown His right to the position by His genealogy, His virgin birth, His fulfilling of the prophecies foretelling Messiah's arrival, by performing the miracles required for His recognition and authentication. He came not in war, but in humility and grace.

On the way in, the multitudes acclaim Him as Son of David as do the children in the temple and no doubt the many blind, lame, diseased, demon-possessed and even resurrected. When, however, He chased the money-lenders and peddlers from the temple calling it *His* house, the chief priests and scribes were outraged and challenged Him to silence those who followed Him. When He first cleansed the temple He had called it His Father's house, now in this chapter it is called "the temple of God" (for the only time in the Gospels), now it is "my house" and in this He was claiming equality with God, hence their anger. At this point He leaves them, goes out of the city, and spends the night in Bethany. It is significant that there seems to be no record of His having slept in Jerusalem. A reading of all the Gospels would seem to indicate that during that last week the Lord "was going" to Bethany each evening and "very early" (one word used means "at dawn") each day was coming into Jerusalem. Luke 19:41 records that on this occasion He wept bitterly over the city because it knew not the day of its visitation.

The next day coming back to the city on the way He curses the fruitless fig tree; surely a parable in action. Again He enters the temple where He is immediately challenged as to the authority for His actions, and it is at this point that He gives them the parable of a father with two sons. They would be well aware, of course, that throughout Exodus, Leviticus, and Deuteronomy nothing was insisted upon more forcefully than that of obedience to parents. Indeed it is referred to by the Lord as "the only commandment with promise", and that promise was that in keeping it, their days would be long upon the land of the Lord their God. Yet during these very days He would be telling them that they would see their land ravaged and themselves driven out of it. So the parable of the two sons would be timely and well understood since God had referred repeatedly to the nation as "Israel my son".

In the parable, the father asks the older son to go work in his vineyard and is met with a flat refusal, yet this rebellious son later repents and does what his father asked him to do. The older son would represent the Gentile nations who were of course in existence roughly two thousand years before the call of Abram. That the Gentiles refused obedience to God is evident from the sin of Adam, in the evil of those before the Flood, the failure of man under human government, and the madness of the age which ended in the tower of Babel. Yet when Christ came He was heard gladly by the people of Samaria, the woman of Tyre, "Galilee of the Gentiles", the centurion and his soldiers, and the thief on the other cross; all Gentiles. Later this would be seen even more clearly in Acts as Peter was sent to the Roman centurion, and Paul would be sent "far hence unto the Gentiles" proclaiming the gospel with wonderful results in Syria, Asia Minor, Macedonia, Greece, and Italy.

Israel, represented in the parable as the younger son, when challenged by Moses at Mount Sinai by having the terms and responsibilities of the covenant (contract) clearly read and spelled out, answered promptly with the words, "All that the Lord hath said we will do" (Exod 19:8). Yet in spite of their prompt profession of obedience their own prophets from Isaiah to Malachi are unanimous in charging them with rank disobedience and even rebellion. Even before the law came into the camp they were breaking at least two of its first commandments.

The Jewish leaders of Christ's day were the heirs of the inheritance in the land from which with tears Christ now told them that they would be driven and it would be destroyed. They were also the recipients of the promises which at that very moment they were refusing and would continue to do so, until forty years later, Paul, one of their own, a Pharisee and Sanhedrinist would be forced to say, "The salvation of God is sent unto the Gentiles and they will hear it." He was quoting one of their own prophets (Isa 6:9-10) to prove it.

After telling this parable the Lord makes the stunning application, that the despised and traitorous tax collectors and the prostitutes were going (present participle) into the kingdom of God ahead of them, or while they refused to repent. John the Baptist, the last of the prophets, came preaching righteousness (the law); Christ came preaching grace, yet they yielded to neither the one nor the other. This was a theme which would be repeated in other parables with the end result added and explained.

At this point it is good that we should remind ourselves of the fact that though Matthew's Gospel is the most Jewish of the four, yet from the very beginning he gives, by divine inspiration of course, hints of coming blessing for the Gentiles. At our Lord's birth the first to worship Him were wise men from the East. Then because of danger in His own land He is taken to Egypt; not only a Gentile land but that of Israel's bondage, to which they were warned never to return. In His genealogical tree we are startled by the appearance of names of four women, Thamar a Philistine from Timnath of all places, Rahab a Canaanite, Ruth from Moab, and Bath-sheba who if not a Hittite herself was certainly the wife of one. Then king Solomon's son Rehoboam was the son of an Ammonite. (Is there any record of Solomon ever marrying an Israelitish wife?) As we have already hinted, Christ in grace answered the plea of a woman of Sidon, healed the servant of a Roman centurion. Then at the cross, when the centurion and those who were with him heard the loud cry, "It is finished", and saw the earthquake and the "things which were done" said, "Truly this was a righteous man, surely this was the Son of God." Surely they meant more than some would give them credit for, and we may believe that these men shall be in glory with the One at whose crucifixion they had ignorantly officiated. It was for these men that our Lord prayed while they were nailing Him to the cross for *they* "knew not what they did" which was more than could be said for the educated Jews who instigated the barbarous act.

Of course the capstone for this whole story by Matthew

is his recording of the resurrection commission to "Go...and teach *all* nations". So in the parable we see in the older son that out of the Gentiles though at first insolently disobedient, many would repent and be blessed, while in the younger son that Israel, though professing obedience, simply ignored what God had to say to them in Christ.

Group 1 Parable 2:

The Husbandmen and the Vineyard   Matt 21:33-44

The first parable on the setting aside of Israel showed Israel as the younger son promising obedience, as the nation did at Mount Sinai, but failing completely to fulfil that promise. The older son, representing the Gentiles, while guilty of open refusal to obey, repented and bowed to the father's command. The Lord applies the lesson though there is no specific mention of judgment or punishment.

The second parable on the subject goes further. The passage is found immediately following in Matt 21:33-44. Those to whom the parable was given could be in no doubt as to what the vineyard represents, who owns it, and who has been given charge of it. Indeed to this very day the Israeli nation uses the grapevine as one of its emblems. The classic passage on the subject, though not the only one, is Isaiah 5, the song of the vineyard. It is really a lament, or dirge, of disappointment. God chose the location, a fruitful hill; He fenced it with His care and protection; He cleared it of stones or rubble; He planted it with the vine of His choice which Jer 2:22 calls "a noble vine brought out of Egypt"; built a watchtower for vigilance and safety, and expected fruit. Yet in spite of all God's care it brought forth bad grapes, and so the prophetic message was that He would take away its defences, break down the wall, lay it waste and leave it dry and tangled with briars and thorns.

This destruction received a partial fulfilment at the time of the Assyrian and Babylonian invasions, but Zechariah 14 as well as many other books clearly foretold a more devastating judgment yet future and of this we have a warning in our parable.

Here a man plants a vineyard as before. A hedge is put around it, a winepress installed, a watchtower built; all of which tells of complete provision for every need, but now the emphasis shifts from the vines to those entrusted with the care of the vineyard, the spiritual leaders of the nation to whom He was actually speaking.

In those days a vineyard at a distance from the owner's home or farm was rented out to men whom he felt he could trust to care for it much as "tenant farmers" did for absentee landlords in times before ours. Instead of paying rent in money the profits would be shared at harvest between the absent owner and the responsible husbandmen. They were not the owners; they simply worked the property in trust, and were responsible to give the owner his pre-arranged share at harvest time each year.

It was a perfect picture of Israel; the land was theirs only in trust. Promised long before to Abraham, Isaac, and Jacob it was divided to the tribes by lot and by name, God clearly outlining their responsibilities. It was His land. It could not be sold (note the case of Naboth and Ahab, 1 Kings 21) and, if through misfortune it was lost to its owner, it had to be returned at the Sabbath of Years or the Jubilee. God had to have His share in sacrifices and worship. The nation failed in all of this as we learn from many passages, particularly in the revivals under Hezekiah, Josiah, and even in the restoration in the Ezra, Nehemiah and Malachi period. In the last named God actually accuses Israel of robbing Him. In other words Israel was guilty of breaking her trust. The owner in the parable sent servants to remind them of their duty but these were stoned, beaten, and some killed. So because of Israel's violation of the covenant or contract, God sent prophets to call His people to a sense of their responsibility. Most of those prophets were rejected, persecuted, and even killed. Instead of listening or learning the nation treated the later messengers worse than the earlier ones. This was a statement of fact well known to the listeners.

In the present parable we are told that "last of all he sent his son"; in other accounts called "the son" and "his only son", "beloved son" (see Mark 12:6; Luke 20:13) and in all passages he is recognised as the heir. Him they kill. This was an act of bitterness and hostility and a final declaration of rebellion, but there was more to it than that. Since he was the heir, they had decided that, if he were killed, they could hold on to the vineyard. Mark is to the point when he has them saying that with the death of the son, "the inheritance shall be ours".

It is not hard, even for us, to see the parallel between Isaiah 5 and these three accounts of our Lord's parable. In the former God asks "What could I have done more to *my* vineyard that I have not done to it?" Here the Lord says, "What will he do to those wicked husbandmen?" In Isaiah the problem is with the vine while in our parable it is with the husbandmen though the basics are identical. The owner seeks fruit and finds only violence, so in the OT the vineyard is abandoned to Israel's rapacious enemies who are used for her punishment. Here in the Gospels the Lord forces the leaders who are listening to Him to say what should be done to those who had so acted. They could only answer, "He will miserably destroy those wicked men and will let out his vineyard to other husbandmen who shall render him the fruits in their season." After quoting from Isa 8:14 regarding the rejected stone of God's choosing, our Lord adds the words of doom, "The kingdom of God shall be taken from you, and given to a nation bringing forth the fruits thereof". Verse 45 adds, "They perceived that he spoke of them."

What a story this is, and how clear the interpretation is! A patient God sent prophets who were rejected with increasing violence. At last He sent His well-beloved and only Son who was heir of all things, and now the rebels are confronted with a choice and a solution. If they kill the only heir, they can make everything theirs instead of the Master's.

In John 11:50 Caiaphas, the crafty leader and spokesman of the Sanhedrin, argued before that supreme council of the nation that it was "expedient ("advantageous", "profitable", W.E. Vine) that one man should die for the people and that the whole nation perish not". His reasoning seems to have been that, if Jesus were left free, He would continue to stir up the crowds as other nationalistic agitators had done in the past. This would bring down on them the heavy hand of their Roman masters and they could well lose what authority and power they had. The solution seemed obvious; kill the agitator and the land would remain theirs.

They left God out of the equation, and history proved their reasoning to be completely wrong. The murder of the Son and heir was the final act of rebellion which brought upon them the judgment of God and they would see their house left unto them desolate. Rejecting Him who came in His Father's name they received, as He said they would, "another coming in his own name". When the first revolt against Rome dragged on sporadically for about five years the emperor Vespasian recalled his soldier son Titus from England, where he had there been putting down unrest, to deal with the situation in Palestine. Leading an army made up very largely of conscripts from England who had been absorbed into the famous 10th Roman Legion, Titus stormed into the land with sword and fire. In AD 70 he broke into Jerusalem, slaughtering and crucifying so many around the walls that, according to Josephus, there was no more room for crosses.

After the fall of Jerusalem a final stand was made by a remnant under the priest Eleazar ben Ezra on top of the rock Massada, but it was a lost cause. After resisting in great suffering for months, knowing that they could resist no longer, the last 960 committed mass suicide rather than suffer a worse fate. No wonder the Lord sobbed, "If thou hadst known, even in this thy day, the things which belong unto thy peace!"

The parable goes further than the destruction of the rebel husbandmen. The vineyard is taken from them and given to "a nation bringing forth the fruits thereof". There is a transfer of position, privilege, and responsibility. It introduces a new dispensation, that of grace with Jew and Gentile made into one "holy nation" (1 Pet 2:9), to which is given the responsibility of bringing forth fruit as expounded in later parables which we shall be studying. This is the present period of the kingdom in mystery with an absent king anointed but awaiting the day of His public crowning.

In Rom 11:21 one very solemn truth to lay to heart comes before us who are part of this new nation: "If God spared not the natural branches (Israel) take heed lest he spare not thee". If we search our hearts as to our fruitfulness, taking into consideration our present condition of weakness and failure, should we not be on our knees before God lest He spare us not? We would be unwise to forget that these parables, though some were spoken to the Jews, were intended primarily for the subjects of the kingdom. Our Lord Himself had said, "To *them* it is not given to know, but to *you...*" This emphasis should become progressively clearer as we study the kingdom parables.

Group 1 Parable 3:

The Fruitless Fig Tree   Luke 13:6-9

From the rebellious husbandmen in charge of the

vineyard and responsible to the owner, our Lord now turns to the subject of fruitfulness and its opposite in the case of Israel.

The context of the parable is interesting. The Lord had been in Judea among the Pharisees with their hypocrisy (Luke 12:1), their greed and materialism (v.15), their luxurious living (v.45), their carelessness (v.47), and the threat of coming judgment (vv.5,56). At this point they bring up the subject of the Galileans whom they despised and who had been slaughtered by Pilate while sacrificing to God. They were implying that somehow such people deserved this, to which the Lord replied, "Suppose ye that these Galileans were sinners above others?...I tell you, Nay; but except ye repent ye shall all likewise perish."

Christ Himself had said in the Sermon on the Mount that "Every tree that bringeth not forth good fruit is hewn down and cast into the fire" (Matt 7:19). John the Baptist had also warned that "now also is the axe laid to the root of the tree".

In the parable we are studying the master comes three years looking for fruit and finding none. There is, however, an intercessor who asks for one more year and the master accedes to his plea for this period of grace with special digging and fertilising. This fourth year of grace is given, showing that the Lord is neither impulsive nor unjust but as Peter says He is "long suffering, not willing that any should perish". It is hard not to connect the three years of the parable with the three years of our Lord's public ministry in patient forbearance now coming to a close in face of stubborn barrenness. The final words of the parable emphasise the certainty of judgment for the Christ-rejecting nation, "if not, cut it down".

One more year of special treatment was indeed given to Israel. The outpouring of the Holy Spirit at Pentecost in the fourth year with convicting power saw 3,000 brought to repentance. Still the leaders continued to imprison and flog the apostles, railing on them that they should dare to "bring this man's blood on us", a strange statement indeed for these very men who recently said to Pilate, "His blood be on us and on our children." The Sanhedrinist from Tarsus, with authorisation from the same men "made havoc of the churches". God waited after the initiation of the age of grace for fully forty years before cutting the tree down in AD 70 with the first destruction of the city and Temple under Titus. Later in AD 130, after Bar Kochba's rising, Hadrian ordered the whole land to be scorched and destroyed. "Except ye repent ye shall all likewise perish" had been fulfilled.

CHAPTER 6

Group 2 Parables

God's Methods of Setting up the Kingdom and Satan's Methods of Opposition

This group of parables gives us a prophetic view of God's plan, His methods, power, sovereignty, and patience. We are also given a clear understanding regarding Satan's tactics for the obstruction of God's plan, as well as his wiles and persistence. The servant of God in this dispensation who does not learn something of all this is going to make mistakes, to say nothing of becoming over anxious, over confident, and at times discouraged.

Group 2 Parable 1:

The Sower, the Seed, the Problems   Matt 13:3-9

It is instructive to note first how different God's kingdom and God's methods are from man's; our Lord probably wanted to underscore such differences to keep His disciples, and us, from copying the world's ways. Those listening would have been well aware of the ways of establishing worldly kingdoms. There may even have been some present who would remember the power and cruelty of the Roman invasion some sixty years earlier. The whole foundation of the Roman empire was the might of its legions. The Jews also celebrated the victories of their own equally-ruthless Hasmonean dynasty which had delivered them from their previous oppressor, Syria. Each successive member of this family proudly took the name Maccabeus or The Hammer. And hammer they did. Indeed Christ's hearers would never have heard of a kingom which was not founded on military might. Egypt, Syria, Assyria, Babylon, Medes, Persians, Greeks and Romans were established with force. Indeed the world system will be so until the Prince of Peace rules from the city of peace, Jerusalem. Yet now the Jews are being told of a kingdom which will rise and spread through the quiet sowing of seed.

The present kingdom of the heavens is a spiritual one. It exists in the king's absence. Its only power is that of the Holy Spirit who was sent down by the Lord to look after His interests during that absence. Contrary to all human experience and expectation this kingdom has been established and maintained, not by powerful armies or by human ingenuity, but simply by the sowing of the Word. Here we read of no human plans, no use of force or pressure or skilful manipulation. No wonder the poet Cowper wrote:

> *How different from the complex schemes of man;*
> *God's easy, artless unencumbered plan.*

In this whole age God's plans have been carried out and His work has been done through His word, whether in preaching to sinners or teaching saints. It has never been done properly in any other way, or in any other power than that of God's Holy Spirit. To copy the world's ways or programmes is to forget the Master's instructions: "Preach the gospel"; "Teach them (the believers) all things whatsoever I have commanded you". We shall never do God's work acceptably or profitably by copying the methods of a world under His judgment.

Wherever God is working Satan will of course not be idle, so the sower is forewarned of possible difficulties and disappointments. The sower in the parable finds different kinds of soil and surroundings, representing different kinds of hearers, but he is not said to be responsible for this, neither is there instruction as to what he should do about it. That is, he is not here told to tear up all the thorns, to remove all the stones, or to spend time chasing away the birds, though he may warn his hearers of these dangers. His job is not to attempt to change the world where he is doing his sowing but to get on with the job of sowing the word.

There will be hard ground, for some are called to hard fields to do the work; perhaps under the shadow of Muslimism, or Bolshevism or Romanism. They are not called to try to eradicate these and other evils but to continue sowing the word. The sower's job, whatever the results, is pursued, knowing that "in due season [he] shall reap if [he] faint not". The harvest results, however are not with him; they will appear at "the end of the age". We can, of course, encourage our hearts in the knowledge that God can and will bless and use what is of Himself. The word which proceeds out of His mouth shall not return to Him void. The sower in the Lord's will and power shall doubtless come again bringing his sheaves with him—perhaps in eternity! Some will, of themselves, steel their hearts against it for any number of reasons. Some may even from "being often reproved...harden their hearts". But it is the work of the Spirit to deal with these hearts and to bring repentance.

The seed may not penetrate here or there and the birds, identified in the explanation as the servants of the wicked one, will soon be there to snatch the seed away before it even has time to germinate. One sometimes wonders if the enemy can use even believers in the snatching away of the seed: for example, at the end of a solemn meeting, if we indulge in chatter about all sorts of things far removed from spiritual things, perhaps a troubled person might find it hard to believe that we are as serious about the message and eternity as we profess to be. There will be those who quickly respond in a shallow and emotional way, but have no depth; so despite appearances they come to nothing. Our Lord experienced this and there is a number of references to it in His ministry. At the end of John 2, for example, "Many believed in his name when they saw the miracles but Jesus did not commit himself to them, for he knew what was in man". Later in the same Gospel we read that after they decided that some of His teaching was "hard", many of His disciples turned back and no longer followed Him. Again some of the excited crowds waving palm branches and chanting "Hosanna" as He entered Jerusalem may well have been among those who a few days later were howling, "Crucify Him, away with Him, we have no king but Caesar." Of course there were thorns which the Lord interpreted as: "The care of this world (age) and the deceitfulness of riches choke the word"; then of course there is no result.

Group 2 Parable 2:

The Growth of the Seed   Mark 4:26-29

We have seen that the basic work on which the growth of the Kingdom depends is the sowing of the seed which, we are told, is the Word of God. Our Lord in this parable, recorded in Mark's usual style with great brevity, reminds us of another fundamental principle which we are prone to forget. This is that while men may sow the seed it is not within their power to cause germination or growth. This is in God's power, and His alone.

This is a truth which we are slow to learn, and so we sometimes try to push or force our hearers to respond instead of leaving God the Holy Spirit to bring to life and fruition the seed we have sown.

Paul, in 1 Corinthians 3:6-9, enlarges on the same truth when he writes to the rash and carnal Corinthians who were putting the emphasis and their approval on certain workers. The Holy Spirit through the Apostle spells out the truth in the words, "Who then is Paul, who then is Apollos, but ministers (servants)...I have planted, Apollos watered; but God gave the increase". We in our day may preach or teach the Word – the giving of life, growth, and fruitfulness is entirely a divine work.

That the sower in Mark's Gospel sows and then rises night and day, simply emphasizes the fact that germination and growth are neither immediate nor rapid. These are lessons we all need to learn.

Group 2 Parable 3:

Wheat and Tares   Matt 13:24-30

If hard ground, evil birds, rocks, and thorns are not enough to frustrate the work of God then Satan will mount a direct attack. Tares are sown "while", it should be noted, "men slept". This would teach us that we can never afford to be careless but rather be on the alert against such activity. It is an interesting study in the Scriptures to consider the frequent occurrence of the words "watch", "watchful", "vigilant", "sober", "diligent", and their opposites, "slothful", "careless", "slumbering", etc.

The tares mentioned here are not simply weeds; they are false wheat called darnel, but which agriculturists refer to as bastard wheat "scarcely distinguishable from true wheat until fully grown". On the writer's desk, is a sprig of darnel plucked in Israel and kept visible at all times in a transparent envelope as a constant reminder of the danger in one's work of what looks like the real thing but is actually where Satan has been allowed through our carelessness to introduce the spurious. We live in an age when bulk, numbers, and the visible are what gains applause and self-satisfaction. Much of it, we fear, will be burned up "in that day". The ears on darnel carry no genuine seed, are almost empty, and have no food value.

In our parable it is not so much a case of trying to hinder the work by obstruction, but to sow confusion, by introducing what looks good but which is the work of the enemy. And it occupies ground, to that extent hindering the full growth of the genuine wheat. It is corruption in its worst form.

Too late the workmen, who perhaps were those guilty of not guarding the field against the enemy, jump in with the suggestion that they should begin uprooting the tares. Our Lord warned against this because, for one thing, they might in their zeal damage the true in trying to eliminate the false. We must always keep in mind that this is not the church which is in view; it is "the field"; the kingdom, the broad sphere of professed Christianity or Christendom. In our day anyone who is not a Jew, a Buddhist, an atheist, or a cannibal would probably be called a Christian to distinguish him from such. Furthermore it is not our job to go around judging and trying in this sphere to decide who is wheat and who is a tare. The Good Shepherd knows His own sheep by name. In the order of the local church it is, of course, far different for here the wicked person must be "put away" from among the Christians, and all leaven must be dealt with, whether new or old (1 Cor 5:3-7). In the same passage Paul asks, "What have I to do to judge them who are outside? They who are outside God judgeth."

Group 2 Parable 4:

The Mustard Seed   Matt 13:31-32

The mustard plant found in almost any part of Israel grows to a height of about ten feet and is a spindly and drooping bush with bright yellow flowers. But it is never a tree, much less a "great tree". Here again we have the problem of bigness which is not necessarily success or genuineness. In this case, however, just as a lot of tares did not make a bigger harvest, and in the next parable leaven did not make a heavier loaf, so the mustard plant became a monstrosity. In Mark 4:30-32 we read that "it grew to be greater than all herbs and shot forth great branches *so that* the birds of the air may lodge in the shadow of it". Luke 13:19 notes that the birds which here lodged in its shadow are now said to be lodging in its branches. The birds had taken over, and we must remember that it was such birds which in the first parable came and snatched away the good seed.

How sad that this has been true. When unregenerate men penetrated the "churches" of Christendom and were given a place in its branches, they became its most dangerous corrupters and snatchers of the good word of God. When such men became the teachers in the seminaries supplying further teachers for such "churches", the circle was closed. It is interesting to note that the word "seminary" comes from a root word which means "seed", and the idea behind such places was that they would be "seed beds". And what seedbeds they have become! The present writer remembers well the uproar there was in his native city in the early nineteen hundreds when the leading professor at the seminary of the largest and most powerful denomination in Ireland wrote an article which was published in the principal newspaper of the city. In it he plainly stated that the doctrine of the virgin birth of the Christ "was in all probability a pious fraud concocted by the disciples to cover the unpalatable fact that in all probability Jesus was the illegitimate son of a Roman soldier at the Jerusalem garrison". There was some uproar but he continued to teach. "The birds" had by then lodged in the tree.

Christ did not seem to be preoccupied with numbers. He

would say to His original followers, "Fear not, *little* flock." The gate was strait and the way narrow and those entering were few. It is true that there were many who genuinely trusted Him, but persecution and slaughter thinned them out and scattered the remainder until some early writers thought the church was on the verge of complete extinction. Then with the so-called conversion of the Emperor Constantine, the tide turned. The emperor's religion became popular; anyone harming Christians was now punished by law; entire legions of Roman soldiers were baptised *en masse*, and "Christianity" became the great tree so that the birds could find easy entrance. In our world, as they say, "big is beautiful" but we should not be deceived. A balloon though bigger than a pearl is not by this fact better or more to be desired.

Group 2 Parable 5:

The Hidden Leaven   Matt 13:33; Luke 13:20

The two accounts of this parable are identical, and for the first time a woman is introduced. It is worth noting that in Revelation there are at least four women described; all of them symbolic. In Revelation 12 a woman is seen clothed with the sun, crowned with twelve stars, and giving birth to a coming world-ruler, the Messiah. She is taken by most to represent Israel. In chapter 7 another woman is presented whom the prophet sees as "in the wilderness" of world affairs. She is clothed in scarlet and is described as the harlot or seducer. She represents the false church of the end times. The third woman is seen as "on a great and high mountain" and she is clothed with the glory of God. She is stated to be "the bride, the Lamb's wife" and she is generally understood to be a symbolic vision of the glorified church. The fourth symbolic woman is found in 2:20-23 and she is seen as *in* the local church seducing the servants of God. She is given the name of "Jezebel" after the vicious, pagan wife of King Ahab who corrupted and ruined her husband; she also caused the slaughter of the prophets of God and the introduction of those of Baal.

The woman of our parable is said to have taken three measures of meal and to have hidden in them leaven. The word "take" indicates a deliberate act. It was not a simple mistake as the result of ignorance or carelessness. The word "hid" suggests the secrecy of the action. Without dogmatism we suggest that the interpretation of the "three measures of meal" or fine flour is seen in both Leviticus 2 and 12 in the meal offering, and in Numbers 15 in connection with the burnt offering. Both the meal and burnt offerings represented Christ: the first in His life (no blood shed) and the second in His death where blood was shed and the fire consumed all. We feel safe in affirming that no Jew in Christ's audience would have failed to make this link. And for this reason leaven, always seen as evil throughout the whole Bible, was strictly forbidden in all sacrifices, whereas oil (figure of the Holy Spirit) and frankincense (speaking of the aroma of His life and death) with which the meal offering was associated, are seen constantly in a good sense. If the woman had been simply putting leaven in bread for eating it would have attracted no attention since it was a daily fact of life.

A woman, and for the first time in these parables, appears as the active centre of the story. Women have a large and glorious place in the NT though none of it was in public teaching or preaching. Mary the mother of our Lord, Elizabeth, Anna, Mary of Magdala, Mary and Martha of Bethany, Priscilla, Phoebe, and many more, must have been outstanding in their sphere. This woman would never have had a connection with sacrifices or priestly work since in Israel only males served as priests; yet here she is secretly, and deliberately, corrupting the meal, undoubtedly a symbol of teaching regarding Christ. Such activity has gone on in the church since its earliest days, as seen in 1 Corinthians 15, Galatians, Col 2:4,8, Peter, Jude, and John. When the German Higher Critics began attacking the Mosaic authorship of the Pentateuch, the date and authorship of Daniel and the very existence of some of the Biblical characters, one perceptive commentator warned that "the waves that are now beating around Moses and Daniel" would not be long in beating around the person of Christ. He was proved to be correct, for soon not only His virgin birth was being attacked, but His deity, miracles, true humanity and deity, His atoning death, and His resurrection were being reasoned away. His claim to deity and equality with the Father were said to be a form of hallucination.

It is important that we should guard against the leaven of false doctrine as one judges sin in the local church. It is equally important that we should guard diligently against leaven of any sort in our personal and individual lives. As disciples we represent Him before men, and we also represent the church to the world; any leaven in us will mar our own testimony, and that of the church, both locally and universally.

There are a number of different leavens mentioned in the NT and perhaps it is worth while to focus briefly on them.

1. The leaven of the Pharisees (Matt 16:6) is identified as hypocrisy. The word "hypocrisy" comes from the Greek language and it originally meant acting as in a play, hence pretending we are someone or something other than ourselves. In modern terms it means a sham, a false front, playing a part. Basically and bluntly it means living a lie. We cannot be anything on Sunday morning, or at any other meeting of believers, than that which we are on Monday through to Saturday. J.N. Darby put it well when he wrote to a young Christian, "What I am before God, that I am and nothing else." The Pharisees made their

robes long, their phylacteries broad, swanning around with an air of righteousness, while they cheated widows and haggled about the blood-price of the Son of God whom they intended to murder. Is there not the danger of playing a part while among fellow believers, while being a very different sort of person in business, among our workmates, or fellow students? There also lurks the danger of "playing church"; of taking the very ground of being a church of God while lacking the spiritual condition and power which such a position demands. Such a position requires not only condition and power, but also spiritual intelligence and knowledge of God through His word, to which in view of our frailty we might add great humility. There is little room for pride or conceit.

2. *The leaven of the Saducees* (Matt 16:6). It is common historical knowledge that the Saducees were avowed materialists who did not believe in angels, spirits, an afterlife, or resurrection. Their beliefs led them to an overriding determination to get the best out of this life since there was nothing beyond. They were, therefore, the affluent sector of the nation; ostentatious, arrogant, snobbishly exclusive and tireless seekers after money and place. Whilst their heterodoxy would be a temptation to any real believer, such attitudes are, alas, not unknown in our day. They are obnoxious in the eyes of the Lord, and really have no place in the life of one who sees himself crucified with Christ and thus to the world. All Christians, true to the Lord and His pattern of life, should be on guard against the leaven of the Sadducees. (We shall be considering parables giving our Lord's teaching on the dangers of mishandling wealth.)

3. *The leaven of Herod* (Mark 8:15). It is a mark of this brood of Herods that above everything else, they were all compromisers. This family, called by Farrar "the viper brood of the Herods" was by birth and blood Edomite, but in the time of the Maccabean dictators they had been

forced by the sword to "convert" by accepting circumcision. Herod 1 had, for political ends attempted to strengthen this by marrying Mariamne the last "princess" of the line of the Maccabees. He later murdered in order to further his ambitions. Then to get his hands on Roman power, he curried favour with the Romans and became a Roman, later becoming governor and virtual king. This is the Herod who sought to murder our Lord in infancy. His descendants were made rulers of various parts of what had been Israel and became in turn the tormentor of our Lord when Pilate sought his help in the trial. Another of the family had John Baptist beheaded, and his nephew Herod Agrippa scoffingly said to Paul in chains, "With these few words would you make me a Christian?" Their motto and guiding thrust seems to have been, "Play all the cards – Edomite, Jew, Roman – for the sake of advantage." In Christ's day there was a political party called the Herodians who were of the same stripe: all compromisers.

For the true believer there can never be compromise. If any man will not take up His cross, say a firm "no" to self, and follow Him, the words of the Lord are still, "He cannot be my disciple." Joshua, Elijah and many others in Scripture expressed the same sentiment. The Herods and their political followers were the jugglers, the tightrope walkers, of their day who mostly for gain of one sort or another would feign "run with the hare and hunt with the hounds"; the betwixt-and-between folks. The leaven of Herod still corrupts in any age, and unfortunately we still have it, even among ourselves. Paul consistently referred to himself as the bond-servant of Jesus Christ, and goes further in Gal 1:10 when he says with scorn, "If I were still trying to please men, I would not be the bond-servant of Jesus Christ" (NASB). It cost Paul a lot to live up to this principle, and it still costs a lot, but the servant of God cannot escape the cost, be what it may.

4. In 1 Corinthians 5 we have *the leaven of unjudged*

sin, in the local church. Being leaven, it will, if not dealt with, leaven the whole lump, i.e. affect the whole assembly. The teaching of the passage is clear; the wicked person must be put away or excommunicated, and this for more than one reason. If left unjudged he will be an example to others that such sin can be indulged in with impunity; he may become a bad example. Laxity in overseers will undermine their authority and bring them under the displeasure and judgment of God. The assembly's testimony in the community will be completely undermined and nullified. The Holy Spirit will be grieved and the whole assembly rendered powerless since He cannot condone evil. In the life of the individual believer it is just as evil, and must be dealt with in self-judgment and confession to God.

5. In 1 Cor 5:7-8 *"the old leaven"* is also pinpointed and condemned as being totally unsuited to those keeping the Passover. This probably looks back to the children of Israel on the night of their leaving Egypt for ever, for it was on that night that they were ordered to get rid of leaven. In our context here it would seem to refer to the baneful effect of judging anything by the old standards of the past life. Both the Lord and the apostle condemned the habit of judging anything "after the flesh", that is by the standards of the old life which should have been left behind. Indeed the Israelites on the same night in which they were redeemed from Egypt's bondage marched out of its jurisdiction in every sense. It is so easy to try to judge christian things, even things connected with the assembly, by the logic of the world and the old life. Such practice is judged as out of order.

6. In the same passage, v.8, we have *"the leaven of malice and wickedness"*, that soul-rotting plague not unknown even among Christians where it would be least expected. W.E. Vine defines malice *(kakia)* as a comprehensive term for all that is vicious; while here wickedness *(poneria)* is the active and baneful aspect, particularly that which is

injurious to others. The two seem in a general way to overlap in part, but would include spiteful and malicious gossip passed on without care for the consequences, or even delight in the consequences. Because these evils are destructive of all true fellowship, friendship, trust, and happiness, they are particularly offensive to God and reprehensible among His people. When some gossip detrimental to another is passed on to a third party it should be stopped right there. R.C. Chapman of Barnstaple had the perfect method of dealing with such malicious gossip. He simply said on the spot to the purveyor of the gossip, "That is very sad. Let's, you and I together, go and speak to the accused person about it." In most cases it ended there. How often, however, great harm has been done, doors have been closed, hearts saddened, fellowship cut off, and service blighted. Instead of this, the person who is peddling the malicious report should be asked if what is being peddled is actually true. What damage, pain, and sadness have been caused, especially when the Lord's clear command is "Go to thy brother".

7. Finally in Gal 5:9 we have *the leaven of legalism* which in the case of the Galatian church made them treat as an enemy the very one who had brought to them the gospel of their salvation. When Paul first arrived there, it seems that he was suffering with some sort of repugnant trouble, possibly of the eyes. He says that they did not despise him for this affliction, indeed they would have plucked out their *own* eyes and given them to him, if it had been possible. The memory of this wrings from him the cry of the heart of love, "Have I become your enemy because I have told you the truth?" He reminds them that he had become to them not only a teacher but a father (4:19). No wonder he agonised and wept. He asks in amazement who had bewitched them into such a turnabout. Hurt and bewildered, he was neither the first nor the last to mourn for this sort of treatment. How many of Israel's prophets

sent for their good and their safety were treated with malignant hatred; some driven into desolation and some murdered. The hard spirit of legalism can destroy the spiritual life of an assembly; it can ruin the spiritual growth and well-being of an individual. It mars fellowship between individuals and between assemblies. It can lead men who operate in a legalistic way into acts of cruelty and even persecution which is certainly Satan's work, while we are ordered by God Himself to "be kind one to another, tender-hearted, forgiving one another even as God for Christ's sake hath forgiven you" (Eph 4:32); and to "have compassion one of another, love as brethren, be pitiful, be courteous" (1 Pet 3:8). These commands are, alas, often forgotten, with resulting estrangement between fellow-believers and assemblies, and many a grieved heart and distressed mind.

Group 2 Parables 6 and 7:

The Treasure in the Field; The Pearl of Great Price

Matt 13:44-46

These two parables have much in common and may be studied together with great profit. Each shows a different facet of the wonders of redemption. They are in the first place totally contrary to man's hankering after size and show. In these we have value hidden but discovered by the divine Seeker. This value has nothing to do with bulk or numbers. Two great truths are prominent and beautiful, the Saviour's joy in the work of redemption and His readiness to give all to gain possession. "Who for the joy that was set before him endured the cross, despising the shame" (Heb 12:2), who "shall see of the travail of his soul and shall be satisfied" (Isa 53:11).

We must not, as before urged, force every word literally else we would have Christ selling possessions, which He did not do. It simply refers to Him giving Himself; not clutching to Himself the position He had, (Phil 2:6,7); but in coming forth from the Father, becoming poor that we might become rich. We must avoid pushing for a literal meaning to be attached to every word lest we infer that the man "searched" and "found" the treasure because he did not know where it was in the first place or indeed that it was there in the first place. We would also need to explain that having found it, he hid it, before finding a buyer for his belongings so that he might buy the treasure. We know little of what He left when He came forth from the Father. We know that as a man He became poor; we know that He humbled Himself and that He had not where to lay His head; we know that He laid down His very life in paying the redemption price, because something precious lies hidden in a field unseen, unappreciated, and unvalued by others who passed by.

The man, and surely as Habershon suggests, there is a hint in that word of the incarnation, buys the whole field. As already pointed out, the field is interpreted by Christ Himself as "the world" and the parable says that he bought the whole field. This can only mean that Christ bought the whole world – all mankind. Here we cannot do better than quote Bellett at length: "Here lies an important truth. It is like a rich man going into a plantation of slaves, and after paying down a price for the whole of the slaves, he sends forth a proclamation that whoever wills may be free. But alas! [some] of the slaves like their little plots of ground, and their earthly ties, and prefer to remain in slavery. So our Lord bought, in His death, all mankind, and has sent forth His servants to beg men to be reconciled to Him, But, alas! men prefer the chains of Satan and the baits he so skilfully lays for them."

This illustrates the difference between buying and redeeming. Many are now deluding their fellow-men with the teaching of universal salvation; whereas there is a wide difference between buying slaves and offering them liberty, and the actual bringing them out of their slavery. We read of some – lost souls whose damnation slumbereth not – who deny "the Lord that *bought them*" (2 Pet 2:1-3). To which might be added, "He (Christ) is the propitiation for our sins, and not for ours only but also for the sins of the whole world" (1 John 2:2).

In the redemptive work of Christ, the world as well as the individual sinner was bought back to God – an area of teaching which badly needs re-emphasising in our day. We, in our natural self-centredness, dwell much on what Christ did for *us*, showing little interest in what He did for God. Our individual expressions of public worship are liberally salted with the personal pronouns both plural and singular as are our hymns. The hymn "Even me; Even me" has seven verses each one of which ends with "me" before the refrain. It is good that sinners saved by grace should thank God for that grace and for the One who died to bring it to us, but surely we ought sometimes to rise a little higher and praise the Son for what He has restored to the Triune God.

In a very real sense the world was lost to God through sin. God had placed Adam in His garden making the man His vice-regent, having dominion over it all, in God's name of course and on the basis of man's obedience – "thou shalt"; "thou shalt not". By turning from the authority of God to that of Satan, man became the follower of the latter, and soon became his slave. This was very evident when God had to drive man out of His garden, separating Himself from him by the flaming sword. The flood, the destruction of Babel, the calling out of a special nation which itself would rebel and be set aside as a nation, the "giving over and up" of the Gentiles (Rom 1:24-26), all testify to the grief of God over His once-perfect creation now in ruin and slavery to God's enemy. Down through the ages God had been robbed of what was His, so Satan is called the prince of this world, the god of this world, and was able to show Christ "all the kingdoms of the world", claiming without being contradicted that it had all been delivered to him (Luke 4:5,6).

Satan, the strong man of our Lord's parable (Luke 11:21), kept his goods in peace until the stronger than he came. That "stronger" one is Christ. He will finally "subdue all things to him [God]" and will then "deliver the kingdom to God". Then, His redemptive and mediatorial work completed, the Triune God shall again be "all in all" (everything in everything). Christ will then have "restored that which He took not away". Yet although He finished the work of redemption on the cross "we see not yet all things put under Him" (Heb 2:8). Hence in Rev 1:9 John speaks of "the kingdom and patience of Jesus Christ". This means that he is in the kingdom in mystery while the absent King and he wait in patience for its revelation and establishment on earth. In the same book at the sounding of the seventh trumpet to usher the final judgments of the vials, the great anthem rolls through the heavens. "The kingdoms of this world *(kosmos)* have become the kingdoms of our God and of His Christ" (11:15).

We must also note the purchaser's joy in the whole transaction as already referred to in "the joy that was set before Him", seeing the "travail of His soul" and being "satisfied". Beside this we have further illustrations in the rejoicing over the sheep, the coin, and the son (Luke 15). There we are told of the "joy in the presence of the angels of heaven over one sinner that repenteth". We should, however, note that it is not said that the angels rejoice, though perhaps they may; but the rejoicing is "in their presence". What a wonderful thought that angels watch with amazement while the very God of heaven rejoices when some unworthy wretch, even a murderer and blasphemer like the malefactor on the cross, repents and feasts in the garden of God with the Saviour Himself – the reversal of what happened after the entrance of sin in the original garden of God!

To these salient features of the first of the twin parables, the second adds its own beauty. Together they may be described as a pair of matching pictures. Here the man is a merchant who knows what he is looking for and knows how much he is prepared to pay for what he wants. The sacred Scriptures tell of many of these precious pearls in every dispensation: Abel who saw the blood of another shed for him, Enoch who walked with his Redeemer, Noah, Job who knew a living redeemer, Abraham, David, Elijah, Daniel, Anna, Simeon.

In the future there will be the great unnumbered multitude of Revelation 7 saved in the horrors of the Great Tribulation. And what shall we say of those in the period of the kingdom in physical manifestation when the great remnant of Israel born in a day will live under the beneficient rule of their Messiah sitting on the throne of His father David? There will also be great masses from the reborn Gentiles who will yet say, "Let us go up to Jerusalem that we may learn the law of the Lord." All these from every dispensation will doubtless be His gathered pearls, yet the parable tells us that he found *one* pearl of surpassing value, and which is of special value to Him. This, we must believe, refers to the Church, His body, His espoused bride now (2 Cor 11:2; Eph 5:23-25) and soon to be His wife (Rev 19:7,8).

Group 2 Parable 8:

The Dragnet   Matt 13:47-48

In this parable we come to an entirely new revelation regarding this mystery kingdom. In the parable of the sower we saw that not all seed sown would germinate and lead to fruit for eternity. In the tares we saw false seed sown deliberately by the enemy to cause confusion among the workers and perhaps hinder full production in the real wheat. In the two parables just studied we have seen a qualified and perceptive merchant seeking pearls, or a man finding treasure which he can evaluate, buy and, for the present, hide: there is nothing false or spurious in either of those twin parables. In the story of the dragnet we have something quite different.

The means used here is not a little hand-net plunged in to catch a specific fish, or even a desired kind of fish. It is a large net dragged, as is done by trawlers to-day, in a wide sweep of the open sea. It would answer perhaps more to open-air preaching, or preaching by radio or television, or to mass distribution of tracts and other gospel literature. Those casting the net are not seeking one specific fish, nor do they have much choice as to what sort of fish will go in, nor could they have any responsibility for the results, no more than the sower had over the thorns, rocks, or birds in the first parable. As with the tares when men were forbidden to attempt to judge and remove the false so here the discriminating is left until "the end of the age". There would be good and bad fish; genuine believers and false professors, until the shore was reached. At the end of the age, the good will be removed and the bad finally burned up. Here the good are removed first, no doubt at the rapture; thereafter the work of dealing with the bad is given to angels, not to us.

This parable teaches us clearly that from the beginning until the end there would be false professors, either put there deliberately by Satan (as the tares), or through lack of understanding, hardness of heart, or frivolous superficiality (as in the shallow ground, hard ground, or among the thorns). In the parables no worker is blamed for this, teaching us that we are not judges – only sowers and fishers. We must also remember that as early as John 2 our blessed Lord Himself had those who "believed" but

He did not commit Himself to them. Then in John 6:66 many disciples went back and ceased following Him. To the very last hours He had a traitor among the twelve. A high percentage indeed! Our Lord never coaxed, persuaded, or used pressure. There were times when, as with Nicodemus and the Samaritan woman, He quietly bore with ignorance or prejudice, patiently repeating His teaching. Instead of "pushing for a decision" with the rich man who came with great eagerness and apparent sincerity, our Lord did not rush to "get the fish into the boat" as we might have done. Instead He probed the young man's conscience with questions, exposed his nature as a sinner who thought more of his wealth than of his salvation. He warned of the cost of discipleship leaving him to make the choice, then watched him walk away unblessed, still in possession of his great wealth. The gate seemed too straight and the way too narrow.

In the same way every careful and wise servant will preach the whole balanced truth of the Lordship of Christ and the responsibilities of discipleship, and will be careful not to push or unduly influence listeners into a quick or shallow profession. "Hath He brought to the birth, and shall He not deliver?" is as true to-day as when it was written so long ago.

CHAPTER 7

Group 3 Parables
God's Ways of Bringing Men into the Kingdom

Group 3 Parable 1:

The Lost Sheep; The Lost Coin; The Lost Son   Luke 15

It would seem that our Lord's intention was to make the three stories of this chapter just one parable in three parts. In v.3 the record says: "He spoke a parable unto them"; in v.8 instead of the usual, "He spoke another parable", or "Again", He simply says, "Either what woman...". In v.11 again there is no word to indicate a new parable, but the opening reads, "A certain man..."

The theme is one throughout, something or someone is lost but is never abandoned or forgotten. In the case of the sheep and the coin they are searched for and could never have been found otherwise. In the case of the son he was longed for and prayed for, but he was responsible to turn his steps homeward, something he was quite capable of doing.

It would also seem that while most preachers make the sheep, the coin, and the son the centre and theme of the parable, this is simply not so. In each case the one with the sense of loss is the loser, not the lost. The focus, therefore, is not on the lost one but, as stated at the head of this whole section, on God. It is God's methods in bringing men into the kingdom which are set out in the parable. The shepherd is the distressed one, nothing being said of the sheep's distress, nor of mountains wild and bare, nor even of the sheep's pathetic bleating. The coin is not troubled but the woman certainly is, as her actions show, while the father's "seeing the son afar off" surely indicates a heart constantly fixed in concern on the direction of the far country where his son was. All three sections seem to be telling us of what God lost through His creature's sin and waywardness. It should also be noted in connection with the word "wilderness" where the rest were left, that Vine and others remind us that this word in Scripture does not usually refer to a desert but rather to open uncultivated country away from villages but open or "free" grazing land. This was where the shepherd left that ninety-nine while he went after the wanderer.

God is the great loser because of the sin of His creatures. To see the mystery of His longing for them and His searchings after them, one has only to read the mourning of Hosea after an unfaithful wife (a picture of God and Israel), or the wail of Jeremiah, "Behold and see if there be any sorrow like unto my sorrow", or Isaiah's "Who hath believed our report" or "I called but ye refused". When we come to the New Testament and read "Oh Jerusalem, Jerusalem!...I would...but ye would not", we believe that we have the core meaning of this parable. Too often we make even our gospel man-centred instead of God-centred, which is a sad mistake.

The Lost Sheep: *No sense; no understanding.*

Among domestic animals the goat, the horse, the dog, the cat and even the cow will either make their own way home, even over great distances, or they will manifest distress in one way or another. The sheep however can break through a hole in the hedge but may not find its way back through the hole again. It will keep on wandering without any sense of direction or of its lostness. The longer it wanders the further it gets from safety and the company of its kind. Yet it never seems to have the sense to retrace its steps. How like the sinner who will blame his condition on anyone rather than himself and, apart from the convicting power of the Holy Spirit, feels no need to turn back or to recognise his lost condition. This seems to be the reason for this section of the parable.

In the parable the action is all on the part of the shepherd. He is aware of the loss of the one sheep, he is prepared to seek it and bring it back, and never rests until this is done. We are not told how far he had to go, nor that he set himself a limit such as five miles and no further. It was "until he find it": love and care without measure or limit. The shepherd does not send someone else, he goes himself. We do not read that he calls the sheep, and when he finds it he neither leads nor drives it back home; he simply carries it all the way. In Isa 9:6 the coming king will carry the government of the universe on one shoulder, but for the security of one lost sheep the shepherd lays it across both shoulders and never rests until it is safely in the fold. What a moving picture of the heart of the Eternal God toward one lost sinner! The sinner, like the sheep, has no care for himself, but the Saviour cares and seeks, and He is here showing to all that this is how He brings men into this new kingdom.

All who would look deeper into this shepherd heart of the Saviour must turn to John 10 where He himself opens up His shepherd character to all who would know Him. He is the doorway to eternal life as well as to abundant spiritual food. He is the one who gives His life for the sheep, who knows them by name and allows them to know Him. He protects them from predatory spiritual foes. He makes them one flock with His other sheep. He is their only master and shepherd – the true Shepherd.

The Lost Coin: *No life; no power.*
In part 2 of this three-part parable we have a very

different situation described. Now we see not a wayward sheep with no sense, but a silver coin with no life and which is therefore helpless to do anything to change its position or condition, nor indeed has it consciousness of either. Again this is so like the sinner. Much time has been spent and lengthy addresses given explaining that this coin has some mystical connection with the woman's wedding or marital status, and writings on the customs of eastern lands have been quoted to that end. Yet the Lord said nothing about any of this in His simple little story. Where the Word is silent we do well to limit our wordiness, however interesting our theories may be. What we do know is that the tiny coin was silver and therefore in Scripture constantly linked with redemption. It was also precious to its owner, though she had others like it. Nine would not do, any more than the ninety and nine sheep of the previous story. Once more we come near to the mystery of the eternal love of God for the lost. There is always another lying in darkness and the Lord Himself "came to seek and to save that which was lost".

There are other distinctions in this story from the others. The coin is not lost in the wilds like the sheep, nor yet among the wastrels and swine in the far country like the son, but in the house. And some have seen in this a picture of those lost within the sphere of christian profession. They are perhaps religious folk who belong to a "church" where the Bible is read, the hymns sung, the creeds and prayers repeated, and "the sacraments" accepted. They are not like the publicans as seen by the Pharisees in the temple. They are not "far far away in heathen darkness dwelling", lost in animism and paganism. But they are lost nonetheless and in darkness just as real as that surrounding those outside; they are where Scripture is twisted or largely ignored, where modernism and evolution are taught, and almost every fundamental truth is denied or ignored, but, thank God, they are the objects of His interest, His love, and His searching.

There are also other interesting differences between this and the other two stories of the trilogy. The searcher here is a woman, and some have seen in this the activity of the church as Christ's representative in his age. She is diligent, concerned, and active. She will not search in the dark for she has a light in one hand, the light of the Word. She has also a broom in the other hand, and thus armed she scours the house for the sake of one lost piece of silver and she will not rest until it is found. She will search in every corner no matter how hard to reach; she will move furniture or other obstructions, and will not allow anything to hinder her work nor will she fear getting her hands dirtied. The fact that the coin had no life in itself shows clearly that it had no ability to help in its being found. It is a clear picture of the sinner's inability to do anything to aid in his own salvation or to alter his lost condition. The story has many lessons to teach us about how God brings men into the kingdom.

The Lost Son: *No submission; no conscience.*

There is an advance in detail with each one of the stories which make up this three-part parable. In the case of the sheep or the coin there was no sense of lostness, no appeal for help, and no word of them rejoicing when found. There was no decision or desire to return, and no action toward returning on the part of either. In the case of the lost son all is different in these and other respects, for here we have a living, intelligent, and responsible human being.

There is also in the section, rebellion against the authority of the household's head in an arrogant youth, with no appreciation of his father's feelings or gratitude for the shared provision of the household. He impudently demands from his father the share of the family wealth which should only have come to him upon the father's death and so puts the father in the place of death as he obviously refuses his father's control. The father graciously grants him this desire and the son walks out, offering no word of thanks for his past or present portion, no farewell embrace or kiss.

How like the sinner this is. How many there are who accept as if it were their right the "life and breath and all things" so abundantly given (Acts 17:25). Yet they ungratefully and thoughtlessly blaspheme the name of the giver, refuse Him obedience and deny His authority; indeed many deny His existence.

The father in grace but with a breaking heart gives to the rebellious son what he wants, and the son gets as far away from the father as he can. Note the emphasis on the words "away" and "a far country". We are reminded of the words, "The wicked are estranged from the womb; they go astray as soon as they be born, speaking lies" (Psalm 58:3). This young man was not only speaking lies, he was living a lie. His father was not dead; he would reap what he was sowing. Truly "there is a way that seemeth right unto a man but the end thereof are the ways of death".

In riotous living he was neither earning nor gaining but wasting his substance. While he had money to throw around he had plenty of friends but these seem to have offered him little help when his money was done. He began to be in want – the word "began" is significant for this was not the peak of his problems, but only a station on the way to desolation. God would now take a hand, sending a mighty famine to the land. Thinking he had found a solution the prodigal sought work from a local farmer, significantly called "a citizen of that country" (of which more anon), but winds up worse than ever when he, a Jew, becomes a swineherd. To any self-respecting Jew, of all the forbidden foods the pig was the worst. Indeed he would not take its name over his lips but usually referred to it in revulsion as "the thing" or "the abomination". Now he is so degraded with starvation that he wanted some of the pigswill to stifle his own gnawing hunger. But even this was refused him.

The young man has now reached the bottom of the pit which he had dug for himself, and God has removed every source of help, and he has to admit his beggared and degraded state, something every sinner has to admit before there can be true salvation. We must note the three steps:

1. "I perish": that is *conviction* as to his true state.

2. "I will arise and go": this is *repentance*; a change or reversal in direction.

3. "To my father", in whose arms he found love, grace, forgiveness and *salvation*: the lost one is found.

The order is clear and plain. There is no salvation without true conviction of sin. Conviction is the work of the Holy Spirit who was sent for this very purpose; see John 16:8. Then must come repentance as Paul preached it in Acts 20:21, "Repentance toward God and faith toward our Lord Jesus Christ". It would have done the prodigal no good to sit mumbling in conviction, "I perish"; he must repent. He had gone away into a far country, and now he must reverse that course, turn around and start off in the opposite direction. Conviction was a first step but conviction in itself would not have saved him from his state of death. He must "arise and go", and this he did. Many seem to think of repentance as simply being sorry for one's sins and this may be one part of it. The word in the original, however, for "repentance" means "to change one's mind"; "to turn around"; "to reverse one's course or direction". In the arms of the father there is the cry of conviction and repentance, "Father I have sinned", and in those arms he found everything he needed.

At this point some important things should be noticed. The young man did not catch his father by surprise so that arrangements might be made to meet his needs. The father was obviously expecting him and watching for him since he saw him "a great way off", but there is more. Both the robe for his covering outwardly and the calf for his needs inwardly are preceded in the original by the definite article and in that language this is more significant than in English. When the servants were told to "bring forth *the* best robe" it was a designated one of which they were well aware, and the same was true of *the* fatted calf. The animal was not merely *a* fat calf, but *a fatted* one. This means it had been previously put in a stall and specially fed to prepare it for a special end or occasion. The word occurs 14 times in the NT, three of which are in the present passage. Four are used in the sense of killing ("arise Peter, kill and eat") but all the remaining seven are used of killing a sacrifice as in "to kill the Passover". The same word is in 1 Cor 5:7, "Christ our passover is *sacrificed* for us". It would appear that the calf slain was more than just a killing for the purpose of eating. This was a feast of reconciliation for which the calf was sacrificed.

In illustration of this we would cite a custom among one of the very large tribes in Central Africa among whom the writer worked for many years. If two estranged parties at last wish to be reconciled, mere apologies and even confessions of wrong would not seal the matter. The parties must eat together (possibly something deriving from the possible poisoning of food). Each one of the parties must bring an animal or fowl of some kind and these are ritually killed. After some blood from these sacrifices is applied to the wrists of both parties, the sacrifices are cooked and a great feast is enjoyed. Without this there is no peace since suspicion would still be lurking in some minds. This feast is called a *chiwanyino* from the verb infinitive *ku wana* "to be reconciled". Very interestingly this is the name which the believers love to use for the Lord's Supper when we, reconciled to God, sit down together to feast spiritually on Christ.

The son is no longer in the far country but he more than just came back to his own country and home. He is at the father's table and the father will be sitting at the head of it in the place not only of honour, but also of authority. This authority he had so much wished to escape from, he is now rejoicing in, as every true believer will do.

Seven things are given to the returned wanderer:

the embrace of love

the kiss of welcome (the Pharisee had not kissed our Lord when invited to his house)

the robe of justification (wrapped in a robe of the father's providing)

the ring (possibly a signet ring of family relationship)

the shoes (no longer a servant, who did not wear shoes)

the calf (the reconciliation sacrifice)

the feast of joy.

This threefold parable, was prompted by the snarling accusation from the Pharisees about the Lord's receiving traitors, tax collectors and sinners, while they themselves refused to come. They objected to grace touching the outcast and would object vehemently as grace touched the Gentile. The younger son, in this case, represents the Gentiles since the subject is place and privilege which belonged to the firstborn, here the older son. The younger one would not inherit the farm, home, and headship, and became through his rebellion a wanderer and a degraded slave defiled by working among the pigs for "a citizen of that country" – an oblique reference to the Gentiles. But the despised one, "this thy son" (the Gentile), comes in repentance and finds forgiveness while the haughty elder son (the Jews) sulks outside and refuses to come in even though begged to do so. Instead of accepting the invitation to come in he angrily criticises his father for not only welcoming the wanderer but worse still eating with him. Compare the Pharisees' accusation "This man receiveth sinners and eateth with them". On another occasion our Lord told these carping

Christ-rejectors that "Many shall come from the east and the west and sit down in the kingdom with Abraham, and Isaac, and Jacob...and ye yourselves cast out..." (Matt 8:11).

Group 3 Parable 2:

The Marriage Supper of the King's Son   Matt 22:2-14

No respect for authority.

This parable and the next one to be considered (from Luke 14) have quite a few similarities. But yet there are differences: differences in the excuses offered for not coming; in the consequences of refusal, there being in Luke no word of armies to destroy those who made light; differences in who issues the invitation – a king or "a certain man". It would also seem that while our first parable was spoken in Jerusalem, the second was given while He was still on the way there, and indeed performing miracles in Samaria and Galilee.

The fact is that when our Lord in Matthew 21 told the three parables we have referred to in Group 1, He wound up with the statement, "Therefore I say unto you, the kingdom of God shall be taken from you (the Jews) and given to a nation bringing forth the fruits thereof." Then in v.45 we read, "When the chief priests and Pharisees had heard his parables they perceived that he spoke of them." Our present parable is introduced with the words, "Jesus answered and spoke unto them again by parables and said..." His answer to them is contained in our present parable.

In this story a king makes a marriage banquet for his son, drawing attention to the fact that God the Father is honouring the Son in connection with His taking a bride, the Church. Surely the prior invitation, obviously given long before the time, was to Israel through all the prophets regarding a great day of coming blessing and festivity. They were aware of this, for in the Luke passage immediately before the parable one had said, "Blessed is he who shall eat bread in the kingdom of God"; at that point the Lord told the story of "the great supper". After the much earlier invitation the call was sent out, "Come for all things are now ready." So after the prophets of the OT, John Baptist came with the cry, "The kingdom of heaven is at hand", then the twelve were sent out, and finally the seventy. Now the long-promised Son and His kingdom blessings have arrived. "All things are ready" for the time of rejoicing and feasting, yet the mass of the nation already invited and now called had other things on their mind. And in the parable they made light of it and went their ways, one to his farm and one to his merchandise, while some treated the messengers spitefully. So it was in reality now, for Christ had come and all things were ready. First there was cool neglect, then hostility which blazed into hatred, ending in the murder at Golgotha.

The one who did the inviting was a king, and such treatment of his invitation was more than insult, it was rebellion. So in anger the king sends armies and "destroys those murderers, and burned up their city". The word "murderers" shows that they had actually killed some of his messengers, so not only they are but also their city is doomed. Such would be the doom of Israel.

The king's plans and provisions will not be in vain, so he commands his servants to go out into the highways and "as many as ye find (whosoever) bid to the marriage". W.E. Vine favours the translation of the word "highways" as "cross-roads". It certainly would be the best place to catch those coming in different directions and this is very much in the purposes of God. Whatever may be a man's starting place or his goals and directions in life, the message is for him. It also shows marvellous grace, for the gospel makes no distinction as to birth, social class, religions, outlooks, or goals; it is for "whosoever". The servants obey the commission and a great crowd is gathered in "both bad and good, and the wedding was furnished with guests". This is grace abounding.

Apparently before the feast began, the king came in to see and probably to welcome the guests. He noticed one who had not on a wedding garment. Some tell us that such garments were provided for any who might need them. A king's palace would, however, require certain protocol and dress code with which this man had not cared to bother. But his presumption led to his expulsion from the feast. The believer has no need to fear this for he has "been made meet (or fit), to be partakers of the inheritance of the saints in light" (Col 1:12). The moral of the story is that if long-invited Israel would not "eat bread in the kingdom", the King will not have His Son slighted. He will turn to the Gentiles and repentant Jews, and His house shall be full. The Christ-rejecting Jews were indeed slaughtered by Titus and Hadrian, and the city razed to the ground.

Group 3 Parable 3:

The Great Supper   Luke 14:16-24

No appreciation of grace.

This parable while marked by some differences from the last one has certainly many similarities which will not require repetition. The differences, however, are significant and should be noted. Matthew who writes with Jews very much in mind, states in the parable which he records that the principal character is a king which would also bring to mind a specific sphere and authority. Luke gives us "a certain man" as the chief mover. This would focus on the incarnation and carries no idea of a country and a king but rather a much broader and unrestricted background, for Luke portrays Christ as Son of Man, as

Matthew shows us the king, Mark the servant, and John the Son of God. Here in Luke 14, there are therefore no destroying armies punishing the rejectors, but for the rejector in Luke the door is shut that "none of those men which were bidden shall taste of my supper". They are forever outside of the provision of God.

We must, however, look at some of the differences, and also at the emphasis in Luke's record. It is specifically called a great supper to which many were invited, indicating perhaps a wider scope than in Matthew 22. When everything is ready, and of course there could be no gospel, no invitation, no free grace as here indicated until all the work was finished and done at Golgotha, the final call goes out, "Come, for all things are now ready." It is the gospel call spreading far and wide the invitation to the great supper.

In the previous parable of Matthew those invited "made light of it and went their ways" to their various occupations. Their very actions showed an attitude of disdain, of scoffing. They were not impressed, much like the leaders of Israel. There were no excuses offered. In the Lucan parable we find a difference – excuses are offered, but they are very lame excuses indeed. A plot of ground is already bought but now one says he must go and see it, something which surely would have been done before the purchase. Oxen are already bought but now another must try them; something like test-driving a car to see how it runs after having already closed the deal. One would have thought that a marriage would have been planned long enough ahead so that when the first invitation was sent the situation could have been explained; or perhaps the bride could have been brought along to the supper. These are called "excuses" and they were nothing more. They had in mind other matters of greater importance and were simply too busy to bother. The servants are not said to have pressed or cajoled; they simply brought the disappointing news back to their master – a lesson for all those who proclaim the invitation of the gospel.

The master now sends his servants on a totally new errand to those who will hear. He is not going to keep coaxing people who are taken up with their own lives and will not listen. Orders are given to go to a new field; not now to the rejectors who, really not interested, were too taken up with their own pursuits. The message is now to be sent to the streets and lanes of the city, usually the haunts of every sort of evil. They are to go especially to the poor and underprivileged, to the crippled beggars, the limping hobblers, and the blind who would probably be begging too. This being done, yet there was room so they are sent out again, this time to the highways (probably cross-roads) and hedges, these last the forgotten outcasts of society, to compel them to come in that the house may be filled. On the word "compel" used here. Vine says it can mean to do so by force, threat, pleading, or entreaty. His whole article in his *Expository Dictionary* is worth reading. It seems clear that God's workers in bringing men and women to the feast will use neither force nor threat, but the mind turns to such Scriptures as "We beseech you...be ye reconciled to God" (2 Cor 5:20). The word does, however, imply urgency on the part of the servants as they scour the city streets and lanes, the country cross-roads, lanes and hedges, helping the blind, crippled and limping to find their way. The servants of the Lord are not requested; they are sent and commanded. It is theirs to obey.

Group 3 Parable 4:

Two Men before God   Luke 18:9-14

No conviction of need or sin; no hope except in mercy.

In this parable we are not dealing with crowds as in the last two, but with individuals for of course in the final analysis God always deals with men singly; responsibility and consequent judgment are individual. The parable was prompted by the large number of self-righteous people who trusted in their own worthiness.

Two men go up to the temple to pray. The word here used for the "temple" embraces all the courts, of which there were three, but not the sacred structure itself. It was in one of these courts that the Lord taught from time to time. There He could have observed cases such as He focuses upon in the parable. Two men are highlighted: one was a Pharisee, noted for scrupulous keeping of the letter of the law; the other was a publican, one of those despised men who sold themselves to the hated Roman colonialists for the job of collecting equally hated taxes. Secular sources tell us that they often abused their position to engage in illegal extortion. The tax collector Zacchaeus in Luke 19 when converted to God, offered to pay back fourfold anything he may have "taken from any man by false accusation". It would have been impossible to imagine two men further removed from each other, but the Pharisee and publican now stand before the searching eye of God in His house.

The Pharisee is full of self-satisfaction. He is not a sinner like others, so he has nothing to confess, but he has much positive righteousness to which he would call God's attention – fasting and tithing. He "prayed with himself" a truly odd sort of exercise. The tax collector stands afar off, probably in a corner, and will not lift up his head before God as he beats on his breast in sorrow and contrition. He takes up his position before God as one condemned and asks only for mercy. The Lord says that the tax collector went back home justified – not the other.

In the short story three things are worth noting which do not stand out in our English version. First, the word "merciful" is said by the specialists to be better translated "propitious". The adjective is from the noun the mercy seat or "the propitiatory". So he is claiming mercy on the grounds of blood shed. Secondly there is a definite article in front of the word "sinner" so he did not say "to me a sinner" but rather "to me *the* sinner". Thirdly he went down to his house "justified", a word very weakened in our understanding of it. Our word "just" originally meant "right"; to be righteous was to be "rightwise" or "straight". One has heard the word "justification" explained as being made "as if we never had sinned" but it means more than this. This would mean that we are proclaimed not guilty, whereas the word "justify" means quite literally that the person in view is declared "just" or "righteous". The difference is easily seen if we think of a law court. A man is accused of a certain crime and faces the judge. The evidence, however, is not sufficient to prove him guilty of the charge, so the judge declares him "not guilty". This, however, is a long way from declaring him righteous because, though innocent, or not proven guilty, he may be a liar, a burglar, even a murderer. When the repentant sinner turns in faith to the sin-bearer not only are all his sins blotted out, which is forgiveness, but he is declared "justified freely by His (God's) grace". Not merely are the sins removed, which is negative, but the righteousness of God Himself is imputed to the sinner. See Rom 4:6 "the man to whom righteousness is imputed without works". This is how God deals with men, bringing them into His kingdom.

Group 3, Parable 5:

The Two Debtors   Luke 7:41-50

No gratitude for forgiveness.

The background of this parable is as follows. A Pharisee named Simon invited our Lord to dine with him in his home, though what his motives may have been we can only guess.

Reclining as they would on carpets around a very low table, with feet outward, there was a sudden interruption. A woman of the town, notorious for her sinful life, entered and coming up behind the Lord began to weep. We gather from the context that she was not simply passing by and, happening to see Jesus, decided to come in. The fact that the Lord had been invited to the home of Simon would have caused a stir, and the woman having heard, got hold of her alabaster container of costly and sweet-smelling unguent, and made straight for the house.

Tears of conviction and repentance flowed and as she bowed down these tears poured over His feet. Then an even more striking thing happened. She loosed her long hair, a shameful act by the standards of the time, if done in public; and putting the woman's highest symbol of glory on the lowest part of His body, she began to wipe His feet with her tresses. Then bowing still lower she kissed His feet. (Newberry says she "was kissing His feet repeatedly" in an outpouring of adoration.)

Simon, who knew nothing of such feelings, rebuked her and by implication accused the Lord Jesus of ignorance regarding her character and activities. This led to the giving of the little parable of "The Two Debtors".

Both men were deeply in debt even though in different measure. Both were without any ability to pay their debt. Both were forgiven frankly and fully, in an act of pure grace. Christ then turned to Simon with a simple question, "Which would love the gracious forgiver most?" Simon could only reply, "I suppose he who was forgiven most."

The Lord then reminds the Pharisee of his ill-mannered violation of the most basic acts of welcome normally rendered to any invited guest in that land. There had been no kiss of welcome, the equivalent of our handshake; no foot-washing, indeed no water given with which Christ could have washed Himself; no oil of blessing for His head. The woman, on the other hand, had washed His feet with tears, had wiped them with her hair, and kept on kissing them (continuous tense). She had also anointed His feet in worship.

The interpretation is then pressed home on the haughty Pharisee. The woman did what she did out of love and gratitude, because her many sins had been forgiven. Newberry points out that the "are" in the text is a past perfect tense, meaning already done but with the effect continuing to the present. She was not forgiven because she had wept, worshipped, and anointed, but rather did these things because she knew forgiveness and showed love and gratitude. Simon had no gratitude since he neither had nor wanted forgiveness.

Should there be any limits to the demonstration of our love and devotion for the "so great salvation" which has been revealed to us and purchased at such a cost at Golgotha?

Group 3 Parable 6:

The Labourers and their Rewards   Matt 20:1-16

Divine sovereignty in the service of the kingdom.

This parable has been a difficult one for many since we are so ready to jump to "natural" conclusions about the apparent injustice of it. J.G. Bellett's introductory remark on it is excellent and to the point. He says, "There is one passage in this parable that explains it: 'Is it not lawful for me to do what I will with what is mine?'" This is God, in His sovereignty dispensing His gifts as it pleases Him. The master goes out at five different times in one day and each time hires labourers; that is "early in the morning", again at 9 am, 12 noon, 3 pm, and 5 pm.

He contracts with the first for one penny per day, the standard wage for a labourer. Later he found others at different times in the market seeking work and each in turn was sent with the word, "Whatsoever is right I will give you." When all were given the same amount at the close of day those who had worked longest grumbled loudly, feeling that the master has been unfair to them. He reminds them that he was not unfair since they got exactly what they had contracted for. What he did with his own money was his business. If he chose in grace and benevolence to give the later workers more than they had earned that was his wish and his right.

The little story shows up in all its ugliness man's discontent and also something of man's jealousy. The first were not wronged; they received that which they had agreed upon, but they did not want to see others getting ahead of them as they saw it. There is also another lesson here when the Lord adds "So the last shall be first, and the first last". The Jew was first, but because of his intransigence became last, and then condemned the Lord for His gracious treatment of the Gentile who came later. It is the sovereign Lord's prerogative to call as he wishes and to distribute as He sees fit. Paul was last called of the apostles, he had persecuted the church (something no other apostle had ever done), he says that he is therefore less than the least, yet he "laboured more abundantly than they all". May we not think that when rewards are given out his will be great? According to our little parable those who complain about treatment or privilege granted to another worker do so because their eye is evil. They see things from a wrong perspective.

Group 3 Parable 7:

A Helpless Widow and an Unjust Judge   Luke 18:2-8

The mystery of uncorrected injustice.

We must be careful first of all to see this story as one of contrast, not of comparison. Our God is not unjust, neither does He answer our cries because He is wearied. He is quite the opposite; who is glad the oftener we turn to Him with our needs, a token of our trust in Him and a confession of our total dependence on Him.

The story is very condensed but when understood it is a real gem. It paints for us in rapid strokes a perfect picture of the situation of the citizens of the Lord's mystery kingdom. Theirs are difficult surroundings in a hostile and uncaring *kosmos* ruled over by Satan, its prince and god. The setting is "a city", usually of all places on earth the most harsh, cold, and uncaring. In the city there is "a widow", the very epitome of helplessness in those days before pensions, homes for the aged, or other socialistic benefits. Worse still she has "an adversary". We are not told what made him such, but the original word means "an adversary at law" which indicates that some charge may have been trumped up with which to harass or exploit her. How often the believer feels in a similar situation in our world! Feeling trapped, the widow appeals directly to "a judge", who is hard-hearted, unjust, and without fear of God or man. She is unimportant and apparently of no value to him so he ignores her appeals for help or justice. The woman, however, is not to be denied and she keeps on pressing her appeal until he wearies of her importunity and, probably in exasperation, gives her the aid she needs.

If an unjust judge can be moved in this way, how much more our just, merciful, and loving God who has also a father's heart for us. There was apparently no relationship between the judge and his suppliant yet she got that she needed. How much more we who are now free to call the God of eternity "Our Father". This is an illustration of the exhortation in the NT to "pray without ceasing", to ask and knock, knowing that our God will never turn a deaf ear to the cry of His children.

The child of God in this present age is a stranger and a pilgrim. Having died with Christ and been raised in Him to be seated in the heavenlies, he has really no rights and must be prepared, as Peter's letters teach, to suffer unjustly; he is to take this not only without retaliation or bitterness, but with the assurance that "so persecuted they the prophets which were before us". Peter goes on to show us that when we suffer unjustly and we take it patiently we may expect a reward, perhaps a spiritual one, while we take our problem to the throne of grace.

CHAPTER 8

Group 4 Parables
The Responsibilities
of the Subjects of the Kingdom

Group 4 Parable 1:

The Compassionate Samaritan   Luke 10:30-37

Unnumbered gospel messages have been preached on this parable, and doubtless many have been led to Christ through its application in this way. To this there can be no objection, but we venture to suggest that it was not originally given by our Lord as a gospel message at all. It was, in fact, in reply to a trick question thrown at our Lord by various groups on more than one occasion. In our passage the questioner is a lawyer, that is a teacher of the Law. Earlier in this same chapter it had been asked apparently in sincerity, though the cost proved too great and the young man went away in sadness.

The question posed on three occasions was: "Which is the greatest, or the first, commandment?" that is of the ten basic commands given to Israel at Mount Sinai. The question supposes that God's moral commands can be broken up in pieces and that men may, according to taste or fancy, decide that some are important and others less so, or even not important at all. We are told in fact, that the scribes or teachers of the sacred Law had broken this law up into 613 precepts, and then proceeded through generations to grade them according to importance in their eyes.

Our Lord in each case states clearly that the law was given on two tables or tablets, the first requiring total love to God, while the second "which is like unto it" required the same love for one's neighbour. He who loved God would love God's creature made in His likeness. This stopped these unloving men in their tracks, but the lawyer thinks he has an even more difficult question for this country rabbi and he puts it forth like a check in a verbal game of chess, "Who is my neighbour?" He is saying in fact, who am I supposed to love in the same way that I love myself? There surely must be limitations, since a Jew could hardly be expected to show love for a Gentile, as the Lord had been doing consistently.

The parable we are considering was the reply to that question, and it was not given as a gospel message at all, but as an illustration of love shown in compassion, as required by the second table of the Law. The Lord was showing that the importance of loving one's neighbour was as unassailable as the requirement to love God in heart, and soul, and mind. This is a high standard indeed of the love I am required to show to anyone who needs it. It requires little thought to see that this and not the gospel was the purpose and thrust of the parable. If it were a gospel message, and if the Samaritan is a picture of Christ who "saves" the battered and robbed wayfarer, in what sense would we "go and do likewise"? Would we go around "saving" people?

The chief actor in the story is a Samaritan, a strange character to portray the Lord. This man "by chance" comes upon a scene while on a journey. He did not set out to succour the man in trouble; he is interrupted in whatever business he was pursuing, and probably was hurrying through a dangerous area. None of these facts really fits our Lord's coming forth deliberately to seek and to save that which was lost, or the shepherd's deliberately going forth to find and save the lost sheep. A Samaritan on the road from Jerusalem to Jericho would not be in his native country; he was away from home, while the man in need was probably a Jew and therefore in his own locality where he was likely to have other Jews who should help. In fact there were two others, not together, but acting independently, and from the very same class as those listening to and hounding the Lord. These, however, passed by cold-heartedly with no qualm of conscience, leaving him alone in his distress, in defiance of God's law which demanded that they love the man with heart, and mind, and soul as they should love God.

The Jews had completely failed in keeping the basics of their own law. This law had never been given to any Gentiles, including this Samaritan. What the Samaritan did he did with no sense of legal obligation or compulsion, but out of compassion. He gave up his time, accepted a certain amount of risk in robber country, used what he had to render on-the-spot aid which would involve unloading and opening up his luggage, cleansing the wounds, pouring in oil and wine (probably in the opposite order – one as a disinfectant and the other a healer); and then instead of making him more comfortable and leaving him to wait for some native co-religionist, he picks up the unconscious (half-dead) man and places him on his own donkey probably supporting him as he walked alongside – no easy job, as anyone who has tried it could confirm. He unashamedly takes him to the same inn to which he himself is now going. Compassionate loving-kindness is a very costly business. Yet he goes further. He leaves him in a place of comfort and safety; pays out of his own pocket for the present, and accepts responsibility for future charges until his return to settle all bills. Most people would have felt they had done enough in getting him there and would have taken a safer route back to Jerusalem, leaving the Jews to look after their own.

This story may, as we have said, be used as an

illustration of all the Lord has done for the sinner, but we are assured that this is not what the parable is about when we read the Lord's clinching final words on top of all the other reasons we have given: "Go and do thou likewise." If this story tells us of a Saviour dealing with the sinner, then we would be ordered to do the same work. If, as we believe, it is an example of pure and unsolicited compassion, then this is what I am commanded to feel and practise toward all men, including one from a hostile race. We do not always live up to these high demands even as Christians to Christians much less to enemies. Yet the word says, "Be ye kind one to another, tender-hearted..." This parable shows us the first of the responsibilities which are ours as subjects of the Kingdom of Heaven.

Group 4 Parable 2:

The Foolish Rich Man   Luke 12:16-21

This parable is the first of three, dealing with the dangers of materialism, greed, and covetousness, a theme often dealt with in the Gospels and indeed in the rest of the NT.

In the OT, material plenty was a sign of divine approval and blessing. Indeed Israel was promised that, if they obeyed God, they would eat of the fat of the land; their flocks would prosper and multiply, and they themselves would be exempt from the diseases of Egypt: "Wealth and riches shall be in his house" (Ps 112:3), "I have not seen the righteous fosaken nor his seed begging bread" (Ps 37:25). Job's poverty and sickness were considered by his friends to be a sure sign of his sin. Dearth, famine, locusts, and poverty were all signs of God's judgment because of unfaithfulness.

As we enter the NT the whole scene is very different. The promised Messiah and Saviour is born in a stable in the tiny village of Bethlehem. To save His life His parents had to flee with Him to Egypt, and when they returned later to Palestine it was to live in a lower class carpenter's home in despised Nazareth. He Himself said that during His mature life He had no place to lay His head, though exactly what He meant by this is not clear in the light of His instructions to John and His mother from the cross regarding the providing of a home for her since He could no longer do this. He had to borrow a penny to illustrate a parable and provide a shekel for the temple tax by a miracle, and He did not have even a donkey of His own for the entry into Jerusalem. A respectable tomb was supplied for Him by Joseph of Arimathea. The signals were in plain view for a totally different sort of kingdom.

Our Lord's forerunner (who was also His cousin) lived in the desert and was executed by Herod Antipas in a dungeon of his fortress palace. His immediate followers left all to be His disciples and from there on would be as poor as He. Indeed the pathway of all true servants of Christ has been the same, whether of Stephen who gave up life itself, or of Paul who experienced "the loss of all things" by becoming a Christian. Our Lord Himself said it would be hard for a rich man to enter the kingdom of heaven because he would have to take up his cross, say "No" to self, and follow Him. It is not surprising therefore to find Christ laying such emphasis on the danger of riches when they have become the main goal of any individual. Riches could become a positive hindrance. The parable we now study concentrates all Christ's teaching on this subject into one pointed story. The main character is a man who makes himself rich in this world while forgetting the brevity of life. Having nothing for the after-life, he is called a fool.

The immediately preceding context shows us a man who though he calls Jesus Master, goes on rather bluntly with the words, "Speak to my brother that he divide the inheritance with me." After refusing to become a ruler or divider of the material things of this world Christ turns to the surrounding crowd and speaks this parable to them. The parable includes only one man, one locked in a little world of his own. He is already rich but his ground has now brought forth even more plentifully. He is like the modern man whose large investments have done better and better, whose business (and salary) are going from strength to strength. Not quite knowing what to do, he congratulates himself before taking counsel with himself. No one else is in his thoughts. He employs first person singular pronouns "I", "my", "mine", twelve times in three sentences, also sprinkled with thoughts of ease, much goods, many years, eating, drinking and making merry. God, other people and the next world would have no place with him. Yet God was watching and said, "Thou fool; this night."

All the gospel sermons notwithstanding, there is not a word here about whether this man had every heard the gospel, much less about whether he had rejected it. That is not the subject of the parable. He could also represent a Christian since there is nothing at all said regarding his eternal destiny. Even a Christian can be a fool in connection with materialism and in light of the shortness of this life and the certainty of the Judgment Seat. The man in the parable speaks and thinks on the level of the soul and body, not the spirit.

The soul is usually seen as the centre of the affections, feelings, emotions: "My soul is exceeding sorrowful" (Matt 26:38); "My soul is well pleased" (Matt 12:18); "Ye shall find rest unto your souls" (Matt 11:29). In James 3:15 and Jude 19 the adjective is rendered as sensual but should be rendered "soulish". This man is "soulish", governed by his feelings. Totally absorbed in the self life, this rich man has no thought for others, the future, or God: a sad state indeed. The same teaching is found in

Luke 16:19 where we have a rich man neglecting the future in the sumptuous living of present wealth. He paid a dreadful price.

Group 4 Parable 3:

The Unjust Steward   Luke 16:1-12

Wisdom in the use of wealth.

This man, like those in the other parables, is handling wealth but the story goes deeper and further since it tells us that even what he has is not his own; he is only a steward. We all need to be reminded of this. The wealth has been entrusted to him by a master who will one day demand a reckoning, as of course He will of us as God's stewards. God Himself has told us that the cattle on a thousand hills belongs to Him as does the silver and the gold (Ps 50:10-12). In Psalm 24 He reminds us that the world is His, just as the land of Israel was His and simply apportioned to Israelites in trust. They were not free to sell it, as Naboth understood. The Israelites were punished and finally removed from the land in judgment for forgetting this. In 2 Chron 7:20 God refers to it as "my land" when He tells them of His power and right to take them out of it, indeed seventy-six times in the OT God refers to it as "my land".

The steward in this parable has abused his trust, mishandled what was his master's, probably using it for his own purposes. His stewardship is now to be terminated, as in "this night" of the previous parable. The steward now decides to use his master's riches in such a way as to make friends for the future and immediately proceeds to do this. At this point many run into difficulties because they forget our earlier warning not to try to force every detail in a parable, but rather what particular truth the Lord is teaching. W.E. Vine says in his *Expository*

Dictionary of NT Words (p.158): "Two dangers are to be avoided in seeking to interpret the parables, that of ignoring the important features, and that of trying to make all the details mean something." Christ tells us the point of the parable in v.9 when he says, "Make for yourselves friends by means of the money of unrighteousness that when it fails they may receive you..." (NASV). This is expanded for us in 1 Tim 6:17-19 when the rich (surely Christians here) are warned not to trust in uncertain riches, but to be ready to distribute whatever wealth God has entrusted them, "laying up in store for themselves a good foundation against the time to come".

Christ did not commend the unjust steward for what he did; his master did. The Lord's comment was that "the sons of this age (the worldlings) are *in their generation* wiser than the sons of light". We too use what is entrusted to us, not for self and the present but for God and with an eye to the future. Lay up treasure in heaven, not on earth.

Group 4 Parable 4:

The Unmerciful Servant   Matt 18:23-35

No gratitude for grace bestowed,
and no mercy shown by one who had obtained mercy.

In Parable 4 of Group 3 we saw two men as they are seen before God. Here we see two men as they should be seen before men. In very simple terms one man is forgiven an enormous debt of ten thousand talents; because he pleads for mercy and time to pay, his master, who was about to sell him, his wife and children into slavery, has compassion on him and forgives him the whole amount. This man has a workmate who owes him one hundred denarii, and, after being forgiven the immense indebtedness, he takes his friend by the throat, demands his payment, and when this cannot be made, has him thrown into a debtor's prison. With inflation as it is today it is of little importance that we try to work out the values of these sums of money, but to give a comparison we would have to say that the first was pardoned about ten million pounds and the latter was imprisoned for ten pounds.

Other workmates see this and in horror take the matter to the master who in justifiable anger calls the merciless creature before him, gives him a lecture on how forgiving he should have been in a small matter when he had been so freely forgiven. He is then handed over to the tormentors until he pay the last farthing.

The whole moral of this parable is that the disciple of Christ who has been freely forgiven all the enormous debt of his sin against God, which eternity in the lake of fire would not wipe out, should ever after, and especially to his work-fellows, be a person characterised by a generously-forgiving attitude. To act otherwise is to outrage the very character of God and to stir Him to grief. We may also take from the parable that such conduct carries its own punishment with it.

One would gather from the story that Chrstians should be the most forgiving people in the world, and very especially when it involves God's servants, their fellow-servants. The importance of the spirit of forgiveness has a large place in the NT where the words "forgive" and "forgiveness" occur at least 60 times, 16 of these in Matthew, of which 5 are in the Sermon on the Mount. Very similar exhortations to this are found in Eph 4:32, "Be ye kind one to another, tender hearted, forgiving one another, even as (that is in the measure that) God for Christ's sake hath forgiven you"; in Col 3:13, "Forbearing one another, and forgiving one another...even as Christ forgave you, so also do ye"; 1 Pet 3:8, "Finally be ye all of one mind having compassion one of another, love as brethren, be pitiful, be courteous". Yet alas! it is not always so in spite of the fact that God has been so forgiving to us. Bitter vendettas can be engaged in for years, even among fellow-servants in the Lord's work, where because of difference, or imagined difference, often long past and gone, hearts have been broken, reputations have been maliciously damaged, and irreparable destruction done to the Lord's work and testimony. This is a lesson for fellow-subjects in the kingdom.

Group 4 Parable 5:

Servants and Talents   Matt 25:14-30

The parable of the talents and that of the pounds (Luke 19:11) are often confused with each other or else the very distinctive differences are not sufficiently emphasised. Having focused on this for attention later, one or two similarities are worth consideration:

1. Both are given on approaching Jerusalem in the final days of our Lord's life and ministry.

2. Both are therefore in the context of His great prophetic utterances about the period of the king's absence and return (Matt 24,25; Luke 19:41-44; 21:1-38).

3. Both deal with the abilities, opportunities, and responsibilities as well as the rewards and rebukes at the king's return, depending on diligence or failure in the use of what is entrusted to us.

The chapters referred to simply vibrate with notes of urgency about the king's return: "that day and hour knoweth no man"; "watch therefore"; "be ye also ready"; "the Lord of that servant shall come...when he looketh not for him"; "a cry...the bridegroom cometh!"; "the Lord of those servants came and reckoned with them"; "one taken the other left"; "he shall come and destroy those wicked husbandmen"; "lift up your heads, your redemption is at hand!" It is against this background that these two parables are given to us. Indeed that of the talents comes after 64 verses of prophetic teaching covering the king's departure, the troubled days with false christs and the tribulation, ending with the words, "Watch therefore for ye know neither the day nor the hour". He then proceeds directly into the parable with the words, "*For* the kingdom of heaven is like a man travelling to a far country who called his own servants and delivered unto them his goods."

So the story covers the period from the departure of their master until his return, a period in which they are handling his riches. Responsibility for his interests laid on each one a very heavy burden. The rewards for diligence would be positions of rule in his kingdom. In a very real sense the time of his absence was a time of probation. Each man was being tested; the way in which he handled what was entrusted to him would decide what measure of rule he would be given in the kingdom. The master would need men of devotion who would work for *his* interests rather than their own; men of intelligence who would make it their business to know and to study his purpose and plans so that they might be working not only industriously but intelligently. It goes without saying that if each one was working within the plans and wishes of the same master, there neither would nor could be clashing in service but rather a "striving together" in accomplishing the same master's will.

The master was well aware of the varying abilities of each, for the passage says he divided to them his goods, each man according to his ability. He was not a hard master who expected of anyone more than he was capable of doing, but he did expect faithfulness and diligence in each, according to that ability.

The parable was delivered to those whom the Master was leaving behind, and that includes us since He has not yet returned. Our Lord has gone away, but He left us with the words, "I will come again", literally "I am coming again". Each one has his or her abilities, all of course gifts from God, but on top of that each one has been given a spiritual gifting.

This variety of gift is emphasised specifically in Rom 12; 1 Cor 12,14; Eph 4; as well as being seen throughout Acts and the Epistles. No two are alike: Paul is not Barnabas; any more than Barnabas is Apollos or Timothy is Titus. Variety of gift does not suggest or allow for competition which works nothing but confusion. In 1 Cor 12:5 diversity is recognised but only one Spirit gives and empowers. There are also differences in the way the gifts are used (administration) but only one Lord. There are diversities of operation but only one God. Do we need to add that God is *never* the author of confusion and where any sort of confusion exists God is not in it. There is also interdependency for no one member can say to another, "I have no need of thee."

Many years ago a little story was told in a leaflet the title of which was *Confusion in the Carpenter's Shop*. The carpenter was absent and the tools were having an argument, each about the short-comings of the other. The hammer was being accused of being too forceful, while he was saying that nobody could drive a point home as he could. The drill accused the plane of being superficial and with little penetration, while the plane retorted with "Nobody can smooth things out as I can." The saw was being accused of being too "cutting" while he said the chisel was too sharp, and yet the pencil had no bite. While the rumpus proceeded with much noise and no work the carpenter entered the shop and immediate quietness reigned while he proceeded to pick up each tool according to its use. No tool could accomplish anything unless it was in the master's hands, and no one tool could properly do the work of another. One has often pictured the same moral as shown in a great orchestra. The variety of instruments ranges from piccolo to pipe organ, but all are needed to bring out what is written in the music. There is no room for individuality here, no solos unless given in the music sheet (the book) and directed by the conductor who is in complete control. There are times for softness and times for crashing crescendos, but all under the eye of the conductor and every eye moves from the music (the book) to his facial expressions and the guidance of his hands. Only he interprets and is in charge. Since the men in this parable were serving the interests of one master it is inconceivable that they would or could be working at odds with each other, much less against each other in independence, jealousy, or spite. Nor was any one put over others as a "boss".

The differing amounts seem to speak of different gifts given according to the master's knowledge of their "several (or individual) ability". Not all are Careys with his outstanding ability in language study, or his equally great organisational ability in putting together groups of scholars to translate the Bible into more than a score of languages. Few of us will shine as a Darby, a Livingstone, or a Moody. We must remember, however, that the reward in each case was commensurate with the talents given, whether five, two, or one. It was 100% for the first two and would have been so with the third. He did nothing, and he actually received 100% of zero.

That man's own admission gave the basic reason for his failure. He did not plead illness, weakness, lack of education, or even mention that he got fewer talents (perhaps because one talent was an enormous amount of money). His failure to gain anything for his master was based on a false view of that master's character, for he saw him as hard and demanding. He obviously did not love his master. The master's reply gives heaven's evaluation of the man and his words. He is "wicked" for thus slandering his master. He is lazy for not shouldering his own responsibilities. He was also dishonest; if he knew his master was hard and demanding, handling his affairs would be a risky business; he might then, in modern language, have put the money in the bank where, without his working, it would have borne safe interest. Since he had not made any use of his talent it was taken from him. Gift must be "stirred up", not "neglected" as in 2 Tim 1:6; else like unused muscle in the human body it disappears.

One point in connection with God's entrusted gifts should be mentioned. When the word "gift" is commonly used by us it seems almost entirely to be associated with platform or public speaking gift. When someone is referred to as being gifted this is usually what is meant; we believe this to be a total misinterpretation. Where gifts are spoken of in Romans 12 six activities are cited, obviously not intended to be an exhaustive list. These are prophecy, ministry, teaching, exhortation, ruling, and showing mercy or compassion. "Ministry" simply means "service"; showing mercy is the gift of helping those in distress, while "ruling" is "leadership" which is oftener done by actions rather than words. Prophecy needed no platform or pulpit and with the completion of the canon of Holy Scripture has no longer been expressed. Exhortation is sometimes translated as "beseeching" which can be done apart from preaching. Teaching may be limited to pulpits by some in our day but there were few pulpits in NT days; teaching was done in homes, schools, the open air, and of course in church gatherings.

In 1 Cor 12 gifting is related to the body of Christ and would appear to mean that each member of that body, as in the human body from which the pictures are taken, is shaped, equipped, or gifted, to function effectively in its proper place. In this passage are mentioned eye, ear, hand,

and foot, all of which we have in pairs. But there is no mention of mouth or tongue of which, mercifully we have only one and not two. When we come down to v.28 we do of course have areas of speech and public speaking. But when we remove apostles, prophets, miracle-workers, healings, and tongues, (the first two already referred to as no longer needed and the other three as having ceased, vanished, or been done away in ch.13:8-10) we are left virtually with the same list as in Rom 12: teachers, leaders, and exhorters; or as in Eph 4, evangelists, shepherds, teachers.

While men of speaking ability are a great gift and boon to the church, some great teachers have not been eloquent or polished speakers. Some have more ability in oratory than in exposition of the Word. On the other hand there are some with a special ability in the one-to-one approach; others are real comforters of the downcast and sorrowing; others in group teaching rather than from a platform or pulpit. The main thing is that we use effectively whatever gift the Master may have given us. One thing is sure, "Every one of us (individually) shall give account of himself to God" (Rom 14:12). It should of course be noted that rewards are connected with the kingdom and not with heaven. In view of that kingdom each shall give account.

Group 4 Parable 6:

Servants and Pounds   Luke 19:11-27

After the rather startling things recorded in ch.18, Luke 19 begins with the public conversion of a corrupt collector of tribute and his consequent offer to pay back fourfold whatever he might have taken dishonestly, as well as giving half of his possessions to feed the poor. It must also be remembered that the Lord is drawing nearer to Jerusalem, now just a day's walk away. In spite of the fact that He has quite plainly told them that once there, He would be delivered to the Romans, mocked, spitefully treated, scourged, and killed, we read in v.11 that because they were near Jersualem and "because they thought that the kingdom of God should immediately appear, he said therefore", and our parable of the pounds is given. The kingdom would not appear, at least not as they pictured it in their minds, because the King would be rejected, and as the parable says would go away "to receive for himself a kingdom and return". The nations might rage and reject the authority of the Son, yet God has set His King upon His holy mount in Zion" (Ps 2:6). His king would return and on this word hinges our parable.

There are similarities between this story and that of the talents. In both, money is entrusted to servants; faithfulness is required; as a result some are diligent, one is not; there is a day of reckoning, with rewards and loss. There are, however, more differences than similarities. In the first, differing number of talents are given in trust to three men; here one coin is given to each of ten men. Here there is an added feature in that while the nobleman is away, his subjects hate him, rise up in revolt and send a messenger after him (a picture of Stephen's murder?) to confirm their bitter and still unrepented rejection of his authority. These would be difficult times for loyal servants working for their absent lord in the scene of his rejection. One more difference is noticeable in that all three of those entrusted with talents are called to account on the master's return whereas here we have a record of only three of the ten being called up, though perhaps they are seen as representing all.

Ten may be seen as the number of responsibility, especially Godward. Ten commandments were given: five Godward and five manward. In the building of the Tabernacle the numbers five and ten are seen in everything except the laver, the lampstand, and the cherubim, perhaps reminding us that the house of God is a place of responsibility. Even in the human body we have five fingers in each hand, five toes on each foot, and five senses, of hearing, feeling, seeing, tasting, smelling. All remind us of responding in different activities.

The three men mentioned in the talents might speak of witness or testimony; "at the mouth of two or three witnesses shall every word be established".

Apart from the diferences in numbers of talents and pounds we notice that a talent was of much greater value than a pound. To attempt to work out the basic values of these coins in today's inflated rates would be of litle help. We do know however, that a penny (denarius) was a labourer's wage for one day, and at this rate one pound (mina) would be very approximately and in round numbers two years' wages for the same labourer; one talent would be wages for 60 years' work, and one man received five of these! Of really only one thing we can be sure, that the talents given represented an immense fortune, while the small silver mina by comparison was very little. It is therefore interesting that the Lord in dealing with the pounds said, "Thou has been faithful in a very little" (some add "thing").

We took the different number of talents to indicate different measures of gift and therefore of responsibility, but it would be impossible to see this when all receive an equal amount. Many years ago now while sharing in a conference on Prophecy with the late E.W. Rodgers, he suggested to the present writer a simple thought which has remained precious and it is passed on as from him. Since the mina, or pound, was a small silver coin, and since silver was the metal of redemption, might the small silver coin given to each man equally not represent the one redeemed life given to each believer and for which he or she will be held accountable "in that day"? The believer sees himself crucified with Christ, and the new life he has received from God is not his own with which he can do what he likes. It belongs to the one who redeemed him so he must hold it and use it in solemn trust: "Ye are not your own, for ye are bought with a price, wherefore glorify God" (1 Cor 6:19,20).

One's life may be seen as "a very little thing" compared with the immensity of the universe, the rolling ages of God's plans, or even by comparison with the lives of the great and famous. One might easily be overwhelmed and wonder what differences we could make or what contribution. All such thinking must be set aside. Each Christian has received one, and only one, redeemed life and is responsible for the use to which it is being put. Ours is not to waste time comparing one with another, leading to either blighting pride or desolating humiliation, both of which would be waste and loss.

Some redeemed lives given by God have been very long; others very short. Some because of position, education, wealth, and background have been extremely and publicly mighty in blessing, while others have had few apparent privileges, hindered perhaps by lack of higher education, by illness, or handicap, or whatever other restrictions God may have permitted. Rather than puzzle over these differences let each recognise that he or she has received what was undeserved – a redeemed life. Each one is responsible to use it for God whatever the conditions may be. The words of the great Christopher Wordsworth come to mind. Please read in God's presence all the verses we give here:

> Oh Lord of heaven, and earth and sea,
> To Thee all praise and glory be:
> How shall we show our love to Thee
> Who givest all?
>
> Thou didst not spare Thine only Son,
> But gav'st Him for a world undone,
> And freely with that blessed One
> Thou givest all.

> For souls redeemed, for sins forgiven,
> For present grace and hope of heaven,
> Father, what can to Thee be given,
> Who givest all?
>
> We lose what on ourselves we spend;
> We have as treasure without end
> Whatever, Lord, to Thee we lend,
> Who givest all.

Group 4 Parable 7:

The Guests at the Feast   Luke 14:7-11

This parable was given by our Lord in the home of a ruler or chief authority among the Pharisees. It was a Sabbath, and the others present were also of the same group. In their eyes Jesus was at best a mere country rabbi: at worst a poverty-stricken carpenter from the despised village of Nazareth in "Galilee of the Gentiles". In such company, He seemed at a distinct disadvantage humanly speaking. One gets the impression that the whole scene was contrived and set up, for the passage says that they were watching Him; the strong word "watch" meaning to scrutinise, as though ready to pounce at the slightest opportunity. There was also a man there obviously suffering from dropsy. Was this also a pre-arranged trap to see if Christ would violate the Sabbath in healing the sick person and thus open up a debate on the Law?

Put in such a tense and hostile situation, the Lord was well aware of the trap. While they were scrutinising He was watching them and marked how each sought the highest seat, probably according to rank or imagined right. First He took the initiative and sprang the trap on them by asking whether the Law of Moses would permit the healing of the sick person on the Sabbath. They seemed lost for an answer, so He healed the man and let him go, but then turned on them with the reminder that they would think nothing of taking a domestic animal out of a hole on Sabbath. They had no reply so He goes on to give them the parable we are about to consider.

The parable shows that the Jews of that day were very class conscious, recognising distinctions between priests and high priests, scribes, doctors, and lawyers in the Sacred Writings. Christ had openly accused them on another occasion of loving the praise of men; they liked to be hailed in the markets as with the cry of "Rabbi! Rabbi!" their rank acknowledged by broad phylacteries and long robes. On this occasion there was an unseemly push for the chief seats, hence the following parable.

What they were doing was, of course, foreign to the very spirit of the Lord's new spiritual kingdom where good deeds and charitable gifts were to be done in complete secrecy; no praise was to be sought from men; praying was to be engaged in the solitude of one's inner chambers, and the poor were to be invited to social meals rather than those rich enough to return the favour. Over and above all the living example of the Master Himself condemned them. He received sinners and shared the meal with them when invited. He preached to multitudes of common people; healed their crippled, diseased, and demon-possessed and then fed them, though we are not told that He ate Himself on two of these occasions – the needy came first. He was to enter His capital city riding on a borrowed donkey. Then when in an ecstatic mood, they would have made Him king, He would withdraw Himself. While masses would swarm to the glorious temple at that last Passover, He would prefer to meet with twelve of the humblest of men in a borrowed upstairs room, knowing that one of those men would betray Him. In the crisis moments of His arrest He would think not of Himself but of His disciples, saying, "If ye seek me let these go their own way", and those for whom He thus interceded would promptly forsake Him and run away.

We know that He endured brutal treatment from men whom He could have swept away with His word. He humbled Himself and became obedient even to the point of death and that death by crucifixion. He prayed for the ignorant Roman soldiers who were only doing what they were ordered to do as they drove the rough spikes through His hands, not knowing what they did. On the cross He did not revile those who reviled Him. Nor did He even silence them; indeed when one of His revilers, in repentance later asked Him for a kindly remembrance, he was assured that his fellow-sufferer whom he had earlier blasphemed would in person escort him into Paradise, the garden of God.

In His resurrection He did not appear to Annas, Caiaphas, Pilate, or Herod to mock them with His triumph; that would come at the end of the age when they would "look on Him whom they pierced"; instead He appeared to Mary of Magdala who would have been ignored as a woman and despised as demon-possessed. He appeared to Simon and assured him that He was interested in having his love, and to the rest of the terror-stricken band with the greeting, "Peace! *(Shalom)* it is I, be not afraid." Though there is no record of His having appeared to anyone not "His own", it is emphasised that He spent the whole forty days before His ascension with His disciples, now called apostles, talking with them of "things pertaining to the kingdom of God". This is the model of humility held up before each redeemed eye from that day to this.

The lesson seems to have been well learned, for every one of those who wrote of Him in the NT signed themselves as "bond-servants of Jesus Christ". In the first recorded miracle after the ascension Peter says, "I have neither silver nor gold," and a little later to a marvelling crowd, "Why look ye on us, as though by our own power..." Paul, probably the greatest of all the apostles says, "I am less than the least of all the apostles." How can we preachers, teachers or whatever else, claim to be followers and disciples (learners from this glorious Lord), and yet put on airs or strut around self-importantly seeking place or attention! Or perhaps the chief seats on the platform? Especially when those words come down to us through the ages and straight from the lips of the divine Model Himself: do not take the high seat but select for yourself the lowest and it might well be that the Master will say, "Come up higher." The moral is that whoever tries to make himself important before men will surely be humbled, even if not now; it will come in "that day" when the secrets of men's hearts will be tried.

In Psalm 1, the blessed man who does not seek the high seat of the arrogant scorner will be made by God like a fruitful tree with hidden roots drinking at the ever-flowing waters of God. This theme is found throughout the OT and is taught in every epistle of the NT. Peter says "Be clothed with humility" (1 Peter 5:5). One translator has suggested, "Wrap yourselves with the apron of humility". One wonders if he was not thinking of that night when the Lord Himself put off His robe and put on the servant's apron to wash the feet of men too proud to do so for one another. No wonder Peter had blurted out on that occasion, "Lord dost Thou wash my feet?" James says, "He giveth grace to the humble." Paul says, "Put on (like a garment) humbleness of mind" (Col 3:12).

Nowhere, however, is this theme dealt with so firmly and insistently as in Paul's letter to the Philippians, particularly in ch.2. Here nothing must be done through strife or vainglory; in modern phraseology we would say "in a spirit of rivalry or envy and blatantly-empty self-advancement". Each must be ready to look on others as better than themselves – not necessarily better in quality but superior in position, an example of which we find when the Lord said, "My Father is greater than I."

Four examples are then given by Paul of what he means and wishes them to follow:

1. *Christ,* who made Himself of no reputation; took upon Himself the form of servant; humbled Himself; became obedient even to and through death and that "cross-death" (Phil 2:6-8).

2. *Paul,* who would gladly be poured out like a drink offering (a trifling cup of wine) on the great and valuable sacrifice of their faith (2:17).

3. *Timothy,* without peer in Paul's eyes, who would care for their state rather than his own, not like others who put self-interest first (2:19).

4. *Epaphroditus,* servant, fellow-labourer, messenger, who grieved because they were worried about his deadly illness, who served others, not considering his own life (2:25).

Let us then, in obedience to the Master and following His example, never seek place, position, or attention, but rather be ready to take the lowest seat here and now, so that we may be honoured by Him in "that day" when He will have us to sit with Him in His throne (Rev 3:21).

CHAPTER 9

Group 5 Parable
A Prophetic Outline
of Profession and Testimony

Group 5 Parable:

The Ten Virgins   Matt 25:1-15

The simplest interpretation of this parable seems to be that unlike most others it covers the whole period of the present kingdom in mystery. Other parables like the sower and the various types of ground refer to the responsibility of scattering the seed and there that responsibility ends. In that of the tares sown by the enemy the servants are forbidden to try to correct this. The only reference to the "end" is brief and simply shows that the Lord will sort everything out then. The same comments apply to the parable of the good and bad fish.

In those dealing with "the grain of mustard seed" and the malicious introduction of leaven into the "fine flour" there is no reference to either a remedy or the end of the age. The same is true of the parable of the treasure hid in the field and the pearl of great price. In Matthew 21 the son who promises obedience but does not fulfil his commitment is replaced by one who, though at first rebellious, later repented. This reveals a principle of God's dealings but goes no further. The same is true in the case of the rebellious keepers of the vineyard who have the vineyard taken from them and given to others.

Contrastingly the parable of the Ten Virgins has its main focus on a course of deterioration, mixture, carelessness, and failure to "watch" expectantly for the bridegroom. It portrays in parabolic form the whole history of the age from possibly the earliest letter to a Gentile congregation at Thessalonica, where they "turned to God...to wait for His Son from heaven", to the letter to Laodicea where Christ is outside knocking and "the coming" is not even mentioned, even though it had been in the previous three letters to the seven churches in Rev 2,3. The background for this parable as found in Matthew 24, we believe confirms this view.

There the Lord had given the longest and most detailed single body of teaching regarding a triple-headed question from the disciples as to "when these things (referring to 23:35-39) would be"; "what would be the sign of [His] coming"; and that of "the end of the age". Each of the three questions must be seen as disctinct, whatever may have been the disciples' understanding. The Lord winds up this teaching by telling them that the final scenes would bring a time of sifting and separation with "one taken and another left", and He adds a brief illustration regarding the unexpectedness of the burglar's break-in, ending with the words "be ye also ready", that is for the sudden coming of the Son of man.

There follows a parable about two servants in responsible positions as stewards of the wealth and affairs of their absent-but-soon-returning master. Neither of the stewards knows when that will be. The first servant expects that return to be at any time, and so is found busy and faithful in his master's affairs and for this is called "blessed" (happy), and is promoted. The "evil servant" is not watching for the master's return but rather *imagines* that his lord is delaying his coming; yet we are assured in Heb 10:37 that "He who shall come will come and *will not tarry*". The evil servant, because of his laxity regarding the master's return "eats" (satisfies his own needs and desires), "drinks" (lives in a state of careless inebriation and unreality) and ends up ill-treating his fellow-servants, something all servants of the Lord should be careful not to do in light of the soon-return of the Lord and the Judgment Seat of Christ.

Straight from this parable (there being no chapter breaks in the original text) come the words "*THEN* shall the kingdom of heaven be likened into ten virgins". It is this immediate transition from one to another which would lead us to see our parable as connected with the ever imminent return of our Lord; the emphasis here being on the virgins' early expectation of it soon replaced by loss of expectancy, careless dozing, deliberate settling down to sleep. The sleep being indulged in by both the genuine and the false may suggest the wilful ignorance or neglect of prophetic teaching so common at present.

The writer's memory goes back to days now seventy-five years past, even before conversion, when the Lord's return was so often ministered about, sung about, preached about, and talked about in assemblies, conferences and homes. Now it is seldom heard mentioned, and in the six years I have been back in Ulster I have yet to hear a single message given on it from any angle. Prophecy would seem to be a subject little desired from our platforms, and it would appear that a younger generation growing up in assemblies seems to have little knowledge of it and just as little desire. We are, alas, asleep rather comfortably along with the godless world around us.

There has been more difference in the interpretation of this parable than any other. Its use as a text for gospel preaching has done nothing to help. Making the virgins the church adds to the confusion since this would mean at least five brides. There have also been hours of addresses and studies on marriage customs in the Near

East explaining what "going out to meet the bride-groom" means, why they had lamps, and so on.

It must be repeated and clearly understood that in this parable, as in those already considered, we are contemplating the kingdom and not the church. In this kingdom we have followed Chrst's work and Satan's constant opposition. The enemy will use his servants to snatch away the seed, and where he cannot hinder the sowing or its germination he will introduce tares to bring in confusion. He will hide leaven in the flour of the meal offering. He will see to it that the kingdom seen as a bush or shrub grows beyond all natural bounds and becomes an enormous tree to accommodate his servants, the birds which stole away the seed of the Word before it could take root. We must distinguish between the church as God sees it, and this wider sphere of professing Christendom. We must also warn once more against forcing every detail to mean something that will strengthen a theory, and we must also be careful not to find something in it which is not really there at all. We avoid many of these pitfalls if we see this parable as a sort of prophetic outline or bird's eye view of the whole period of the Kingdom from first to last.

In this parable, all begins with a bright period when heart and mind were set on "the coming", as represented by the ten who go out to meet Him. As W. Kelly says, they go out leaving all else behind as Christians should. It is not long before we become aware that mixture has crept in, for we are told immediately that "five of them were wise, and five foolish". They have their lamps with them and seem full of happy expectancy. Soon, however, they feel the bridegroom is tarrying and the expectancy dies. They probably sit down, for shortly they begin to doze or nod (slumber), and finally make themselves comfortable, settling down to sleep. Then comes the midnight cry, an arousing, the exposure of lack of reality; then the bridegroom comes and the door is shut.

There would seem to be six periods predicted, in the parable, four of which have been fulfilled, and two are yet to be. We shall first follow the four fulfilled ones historically.

1. See v. 1. The earliest days of the age of grace were full of bright expectation regarding the coming of the Lord to remove His people. They saw Him as absent but soon coming. Every writer of NT Epistles holds this coming before the eyes of the Christians as "the blessed hope": whether Paul, James, Peter, Jude, John, or the writer to the Hebrews. From many occurrences a selection with illustrate:

Paul: "Now is our salvation nearer than when we believed"; "Waiting for the blessed hope"; "The dead in Christ shall rise first"; "In a moment...the dead shall be raised and we shall be changed"; "We which are alive and remain shall be caught up".

Hebrews: "And so much the more as ye see the day approaching".

James: "Be patient brethren unto the coming of the Lord".

Peter: "The day of the Lord will come as a thief".

John: "When He shall appear we shall be like Him"; "Behold I come quickly".

Jude: "The Lord cometh with ten thousands of His saints".

The early believers, however new in the faith, as in Thessalonica for example, were pilgrims awaiting "the coming". This early period answers to the opening of the parable: "They took their lamps and went out to meet the bridegroom".

2. See v.2. Mixed conditions soon become apparent: "five were wise and five were foolish". In other parables we see tares, bad fish, wicked servants beating their fellow-servants, drunken servants. So we read in the NT "they went out...they were not of us", "wicked men...crept in

unawares", "foolish Galatians, who hath bewitched you...let him be accursed", "even now are there many anti-christs"; "thou hast there that woman Jezebel". These show how early in the first century admixture started. This reached new heights under Constantine when with the Emperor's so-called conversion the world came into the church as we have already noticed.

All the virgins had lamps, but whereas the wise took oil with their lamps the foolish *had no oil.* This fact should be clearly understood since some carelessly say that they had oil in their lamps but no extra oil. The fact is that the word for "lamp" here is really a torch and not a lamp with oil and a wick. Writers on the ways and customs of the Holy Land have described these torches as poles with a tightly-bound bunch of some brush-like material tied on top. There was no tank or container of oil. The torch would be soaked in thick oil, wax, or other semi-liquid flammable material and this would have to be replenished after a time. The foolish girls simply had "no oil with them".

3. See v.5. "While the bridegroom tarried they all slumbered and slept": answers to the third period of the kingdom age. We must first notice the word "tarry" here, which only occurs four times elsewhere in the NT. The first two are in the same parable recorded in Matt 24:48 and Luke 12:45 which have, "if that evil (or wicked) servant say in his heart, My Lord *delayeth* his coming". In Luke 1:21, "the people wondered that he (Zecharias) *delayed*". In each of these cases it is not stated that the person involved actually delayed but that he was thought or seemed to be delaying. The fifth passage, Heb 10:37, clearly states that "He that shall come will come, and will *not tarry*". From these we gather that the virgins thought or felt that the bridegroom was tarrying, so the eager expectancy gradually faded. They would seem to have sat down for they slumbered and slept. The feeling or supposition that the bridegroom tarried led to a dangerous

attitude. They lost, as the early Christians soon did, the sense of the imminence of the bridegroom's coming. Indeed especially after Constantine's "conversion" when persecution stopped and the church was progressively modelled on the Empire, many imagined that Christ's visible kingdom would be brought about through christian activity. The "hope of His coming" was then completely lost and only centuries later was it rediscovered.

A hymn very popular in many places and which begins with, "We've a story to tell to the nations", goes on to say, "For the darkness shall turn to dawning and the dawning to noonday bright, and God's great kingdom shall come on earth..." This kind of thing was of course mixed up with the concept of a "general judgment at the last day" when we would find out whether or not we were good enough to go to heaven. The Reformation, great and blessed though it was, did not revive or rediscover the truth of the coming of Christ to the air to call away the church (1 Thess 4:16; 1 Cor 15:51,52). Sir Robert Anderson refers to a mass of commentaries up to a certain point (and some continuing to-day) giving the impression that the "last days will be a general pandemonium ending in a bonfire". The above hymn, though set to wonderfully attractive music, should long since have been purged from our hymnbooks. The gospel is not, and never was, the means of bringing about "God's great kingdom of love and light". That will be done by the Lord's coming in judgment and fiery indignation. The message we have is not for converting nations but for calling out sinners *from* the nations to form something distinct, namely the Church.

There had been mockers even in Peter's days who taunted with the words, "Where is the promise of His coming?" (2 Pet 3:4), to which he gives the answer, "God is not slack concerning his promise", and indeed one chapter earlier he had said of such people "Their judgment slumbereth not", that is, it was certain to come.

4. See vv.6-9. Now in our parable we read that at midnight there was a cry made, "Behold the bridegroom cometh; go ye out to meet him." Many feel that this indicates that the bridegroom actually came at that point, but in His coming He is called "the bright and *morning* star" (Rev 22:16), which would seem to indicate that His coming will introduce the dawn and not midnight. It is not said that the bridegroom came when the cry was made. We find in fact that there was time for consultation among them as the cry brought home the truth of his coming and they began to trim their lamps; time even for the foolish ones to go searching for oil.

This cry is seen by some, among them very reliable commentators, to refer rather to a time when about 170 years ago in the early 19th century the truth of the Rapture was re-discovered, the coming to the air of the Bridegroom to call away His bride. This rediscovery had a tremendous impact on the christian world and indeed played a great part in the revivals immediately after that time. For that Rapture no date was announced; it was seen as something which could take place at any time and it caused an awakening among evangelical believers – a cry in the midnight darkness when many believers were spiritually asleep. It also was taken advantage of in a perverted way by Adventists, Mormons, Christian Scientists, and other cults, each in their own way and for their own ends. Satan has an answer for every movement of God.

The fact that all ten virgins had dozed and finally slept is a dreadful reflection on true believers asleep, and without much visible difference between them and a world sleeping on the brink of judgment and doom. Now there is a sudden scramble for they are caught "unawares" (Luke 21:34). At last the unwise become aware that in spite of all efforts their torches have gone out and no amount of trimming will solve the problem. An appeal to their fellows is fruitless as it must ever be, for human aid is of no help in this extremity.

At this point we now come to the two prophetic statements which have yet to be fulfilled.

5. See v.10. The Bridegroom came; those ready not only went in to the wedding banquet but "went in with Him". This is the marriage supper of the Lamb referred to in Rev 19.

6. See vv.10-13. "The door was shut", announced the end of opportunity for those who are not ready. With the removal of the church there is no more hope for those who have rejected Christ: "they received not the love of the truth that they might be saved, and for this cause God shall send them strong delusion that they should believe the lie that they all might be judged who believed not the truth, but had pleasure in unrighteousness" (2 Thess 2:10). Inside there shall be eternal bliss and joy. Once the door is shut, however, there is nothing but weeping and wailing and gnashing of teeth.

Supposing we heard to-day for the first time of the coming of our Lord to snatch away all the true-born believers; that they were to be caught away; to be transformed into the likeness of His body of glory; to be eternally with Him, to worship in perfection with no tears, no sickness, no death; to share eternal bliss with Him. Would it not transform our lives? Why then does it not do this to us now?

CHAPTER 10

Lessons for Daily Living

We have shown that all the parabolic teaching of our Lord followed upon His rejection by Israel, His pronouncement of divine judgment on that nation, and His clear statements about turning to those who would "bring forth the fruits thereof". This clearly introduces the present age of grace and a new spiritual kingdom open to both Jew and Gentile on that ground and by faith alone. That age is indicated as continuing until the Lord's return, whether in the Rapture to remove the church, or in the subsequent coming in judgment and glory to establish His millennial kingdom. That we are part of this present "kingdom in mystery" should be clear by such terms as "Ye are a holy nation" (1 Pet 2:9) and our having been brought into "the kingdom of [God's] dear son". Therefore the positive teachings of these parables are for us, right from the earliest, the sowing of the seed, to the final one, the closing of the door in the parable of the ten virgins. This parable is really the only one which covers the whole period, hence its importance.

Some may *apply* the parables in a gospel sense; and no objection should be raised to this, but each has a message of such importance for us that anything which would blunt its edge for present day believers must be avoided. Each is of immense importance for Christians in such a day as ours. In the light of this importance and responsibility, we conclude by summarising and reviewing the demands laid upon us in all these parables:

The two sons: What is demanded of us is unquestioning obedience; otherwise we come under His condemnation (John 8:31; Rom 6:16).

The vineyard and the husbandmen: The test is fidelity: if we take the place of those so honoured in this age then nothing short of total fidelity will satisfy God.

The fruitless fig tree: Self-examination as to the fruitfulness of our lives is called for. It should be noted that whereas under this heading we almost exclusively think of fruitfulness in terms of "souls led to Christ", the Holy Spirit clearly states that "the fruit of the Spirit is love, joy, peace, longsuffering, gentleness, goodness, faith, meekness, temperance (self-control)". This is surely a pen picture of the character of Christ the vine, which should be reproduced in us the branches. Read carefully and humbly Eph 5:9; Phil 1:11; Jas 3:17-18; and especially Rom 11:21, "If God spared not the natural branches (Israel) take heed lest He also spare not thee".

The sower: Our duty is to be constantly sowing the seed of the word, and leaving the results with Him since we are assured that only His sovereign power produces germination (Mark 4:26-29).

The tares: We must always be aware that we have a crafty enemy who would seek to deceive us into the acceptance of counterfeit instead of reality.

The mustard seed, the leaven in the meal: We learn that we must never mistake the big for the genuine or valuable in God's eyes. With regard to the latter we must also be on our guard against any false doctrine (leaven) especially in connection with the person of Christ (the true Meal Offering).

The two men in the temple: We must avoid and abhor any sort of self-conceit or pride (Luke 18:10) whether in salvation or in christian living.

The hid treasure, the pearl of great price: Whatever Christ treasures we should count of greatest value, and worship

Him for seeking, finding, and purchasing it.

The two debtors: Having been forgiven much we should love much, and also be prepared to forgive others, as the parable of *the unmerciful servant* shows.

The lost sheep, coin, and son: This parable shows beyond doubt the sense of loss on the part of the Lord. We have also His loving, tireless, and self-sacrificing seeking and providing until what was lost is restored. Should this not also characterise us if we have His Spirit and His love for the lost?

The great supper and *the king's marriage banquet:* We are under obligation to obey His command to go out into the streets, highways, lanes, and crossroads, and in love to urge in to the feast the lame, wounded, poor, and blind.

The widow and the unjust judge: The value of perseverance in prayer, something needed by all, and often a point of grave failure.

The compassionate Samaritan: "Go thou and do likewise" is the challenge. A Christian saved from a life of sin and a place in the Lake of Fire should be the most compassionate person in the world. Yet some of us seem to find it hard to be compassionate even to a fellow-believer.

The foolish rich man, the unjust steward, the unmerciful servant: All emphasise the fact that while in the OT riches and prosperity were a sign of divine approval, in the present age material prosperity can and may become a source of hindrance and even danger if not properly handled, or if it should become the goal of one's life.

Talents and pounds: Gift, abilities, and responsibilities from an absent-but-soon-returning master bring responsibility in view of the judgment seat of Christ.

The wise and foolish virgins: This survey of the whole history of the kingdom in mystery period requires a sober examining of our hearts before God. It raises questions.

Is there not mixture, not only of individuals but of motives? Have we the same burning consciousness of the immediacy of the Lord's return that saints once had?